Methodological Challenges When Exploring Digital Learning Spaces in Education

NEW RESEARCH – NEW VOICES

Volume 2

New Research – New Voices involves two strands, leaving open the possibility of others as the series grows:

Strand 1: New Voices and New Knowledge in Research Methodology
This strand in the book series is dedicated to producing cutting-edge titles focusing on Research Methodology. While it might be generally acknowledged that educational researchers often tend to import methods developed in neighboring disciplines, this is not always acknowledged in the literature on methodology. This series intends to contribute to the knowledge foundation in educational research by specifically seeking out those who work both across disciplines and inter-disciplinary in terms of their methodological approaches. The overall focus is to develop a series focusing on those methods which are appropriate in dealing with the specific research problems of the discipline.

The series provides students and scholars with state-of-the-art scholarship on methodology, methods and techniques focusing on a range of research topics. It comprises innovative and intellectually rigorous monographs and edited collections which bridge schools of thought and cross the boundaries of conventional approaches. The series covers a broad range of issues focusing on not only empirical-analytical and interpretive approaches, but moreover on micro and macro studies, and quantitative and qualitative methods.

Strand 2: New Voices and New Knowledge in Educational Research
This part of the series will focus on theoretical and empirical contributions that are unique and will provide important insights into the field of educational research across a range of contexts globally. This part of the series will collectively communicate new voices, new insights and new possibilities within the field of educational research. In particular the focus will be on scholars, students and communities that have often been excluded or marginalized within educational research and practice.

Methodological Challenges When Exploring Digital Learning Spaces in Education

Edited by

Greta Björk Gudmundsdottir
The Norwegian Centre for ICT in Education
Oslo, Norway

and

Kristin Beate Vasbø
Department of Teacher Education and School Research
University of Oslo, Norway

SENSE PUBLISHERS
ROTTERDAM / BOSTON / TAIPEI

A C.I.P. record for this book is available from the Library of Congress.

ISBN 978-94-6209-735-3 (paperback)
ISBN 978-94-6209-736-0 (hardback)
ISBN 978-94-6209-737-7 (e-book)

Published by: Sense Publishers,
P.O. Box 21858, 3001 AW Rotterdam, The Netherlands
https://www.sensepublishers.com/

Printed on acid-free paper

TABLE OF CONTENTS

PART IV: CHALLENGES AHEAD

ACKNOWLEDGEMENTS

The editors would like to express their great appreciation to many people who have played a part in bringing this volume to completion. We would like to acknowledge the authors for their contributions, and for their hard work and enthusiasm. All the manuscripts went through a thorough peer-review process and the authors refined their chapters to the final form presented here. The result is a volume that provides a variety of approaches and professional aspects in terms of methodological challenges when using ICT in educational research.

We are also most grateful to all the reviewers for their comprehensive peer reviews and valuable comments. Their constructive feedback and suggestions contributed to improved quality of this publication.

We furthermore owe a debt of gratitude to the series editor Professor Halla Holmarsdottir for her continuous support and encouragement. We are also grateful to Michel Lokhorst and the staff of Sense Publishers, Rotterdam, the Netherlands, who took responsibility for the production process.

We hope that this volume will be useful and valuable for you as a researcher, graduate student or as a person particularly interested in methodological issues and ICT in various learning spaces.

KRISTIN BEATE VASBØ AND GRETA BJÖRK GUDMUNDSDOTTIR

1. METHODOLOGICAL CHALLENGES WHEN EXPLORING NEW LEARNING SITES IN EDUCATIONAL RESEARCH

INTRODUCTION

In a variety of educational contexts today, educators, policy-makers and researchers are turning to ICT-based practices to design learning materials, to structure educational methods, to enhance learning outcomes and experiences, and to develop new approaches in supporting teaching and learning (Athanassios, 2012; Laurillard, 2012; Price, Jewitt, & Brown, 2013a; Punie & Ala-Mutka, 2007). Empowered by technology, students and teachers are turning established teaching models on their heads by "flipping the classroom", while new skills and demands from the work environment are redefining the emphasis within educational institutions. Moreover, digital media is perceived as a catalyst for new forms of knowledge production by facilitating a variety of opportunities to share content and resources (Drotner, 2013; Sefton-Green, 2013; Leander, Phillips, & Taylor, 2010).

Due to their access to the Internet and a variety of low-cost digital authoring tools, young people today have a broader social and technological repertoire to engage in self-authoring and digital media production (Ito et al., 2013; Ito, 2009). A person with a smartphone has instantaneous access to millions of articles, books, essays, academic research, lectures and courses on every imaginable subject. This development has broken down the barriers that used to exist between knowledge and schools and libraries that were the gatekeepers of knowledge. Young people live in an interactive culture characterized by unlimited access to information and content – anytime, anywhere. Digital media and networks have become a "taken for granted" part of our everyday lives, and thus, provide alternative approaches to how we engage in learning, communication and creative expression (Erstad, 2012; Furlong & Davies, 2012; Miller & Horst, 2012; Ito et al., 2010; Buckingham, 2008; Gee, 2004; Leander et al., 2010). The point of departure of this volume is the question of how we can approach and develop our research methodology in educational research in order to cope with the new digital environment we are facing.

Over the last decade, the practices by which scholarly knowledge is produced – both within and across disciplines – have been substantially influenced by the appearance of digital information resources, communication networks and technology enhanced research tools. Viewed from a methodological perspective, the rich ICT-based environment in educational settings influences research methods, ethics and the general conduct of research. Digital videos and multimedia

G.B. Gudmundsdottir and K.B. Vasbø (Eds.), Methodological Challenges When Exploring Digital Learning Spaces in Education, 1–9.

make it possible to capture and share much richer records of human action and context, enabling a flexible analysis not only of static artifacts and talk, but also a spectrum of symbolic and physical interactions, including gestures, movements in space and changes over time. The possibilities within these new forms of data are numerous, but at the same time the digitisation of data and other technological developments create new methodological challenges. Although there are rapid shifts in technical development and the types of devices, networks and practices that people engage in, the theoretical and methodological approaches to the pedagogical use of digital technology are developing at a much slower pace (Price, Jewitt, & Brown, 2013b). When we conduct research on current learning practices as they unfold, across and between online and offline contexts, both in an empirically and a methodological sense, our research skills, tools and strategies are put to the test.

This volume is devoted to stimulating debate about the various methodological challenges facing the researcher in the digital sphere of educational research, and furthermore, exploring what kind of new methodological approaches these challenges impose. From various perspectives, the chapters deal with three particularly demanding challenges for educational research in digital learning contexts. The first challenge concerns how research manages to explore networked learning within a multi-faceted ICT environment. What kind of research designs and forms of data collection are able to grasp this complexity of multiple learning taking place within these contexts? The second challenge deals with how researchers experience the research context and interact with various actors within these settings. How to capture and understand interaction between contexts and across different dimensions of contexts in time and space? And finally, the third challenge is about exploring how children make meaning across physical places and virtual spaces. How can researchers manage to analyse processes of meaning making, as they play out simultaneously both online and offline? How to capture learning taking place between contexts? All together, these challenges are questioning the traditional focus on physical places in educational research as the main site for research (Leander et al., 2010). Furthermore, they are questioning the traditional research methods that we use and are familiar with.

New Perspectives on Learning and Space

Over the past 20 years, interest in spatial aspects of human life and social relations has become widespread in a variety of academic disciplines including education (Leander et al., 2010). Perspectives of what the notion of space entails have varied across different authors (Savin-Baden & Howell Major, 2010), and a broad variety of discussions concerning space have become more evident in educational research, challenging established frameworks, theories and practices (Kalervo, 2011). The term "spatial turn" was introduced by the human geographer Edward Soja (1996) who argued for real and imagined spaces to be brought together. On account of Soja's contribution, among others, space is now acknowledged across the disciplines as a formidable force that shapes human actions. Whereas space was previously thought of as empty, available and waiting to be filled up, recent theories have revealed that space is a product and process of socially dynamic relations that shape our lives in various ways (Sheehy & Leander, 2004; Pink, 2012).

Space and spatiality are seen as active and formative processes developing over time. The new idea of spatiality of human life separates places from their location, and place is understood in terms of movement and relationships. Furthermore, Moje (2004) claims that material spaces and places shape and reflect our identity and literacy practices. Historically, the field of learning has had a top-down approach, but this is being turned on its head. According to Leander et al. (2010), there is an emergent agenda in educational research for studying students' learning across space and time in an interdisciplinary way. In this volume, we are inspired by this perspective, and the contributors originate from a wide range of subdivisions within educational research using various methodological approaches. By challenging the perception of the "classroom as a container" for learning, which is a traditional understanding within educational research, Leander et al. introduce an alternative perspective opening up the classroom, by introducing the expression "a node in a network" as a metaphor for the new classroom. The role of new technologies is to support the alternative discourse provided by Leander et al. focusing on themes like learning in place, learning trajectories, learning networks, learning geographies and mobility. Following this line of thinking, digital media serve to further disperse and transform arenas of learning because they are not bound to specific localities, spaces or times of use. The new dynamic perspective of space also strongly affects how we conduct research on learning (Leander et al., 2010; Sheehy & Leander, 2004; Savin-Baden & Howell Major, 2010). Once the concepts and phenomena we want to study are fluid and changing, our research focus and tools need to become unsettled and capable of moving between and across multiple spaces. The chapters in this volume present different angles problematizing how we can capture, explore and understand how learning and meaning making take place across different dimensions of contexts in time and space.

The Multi-Sited Context of Research

Digital technology has been applied, adapted and integrated in existing approaches and established qualitative research methodologies. However, researchers are faced with challenges about what it means to be a qualitative researcher in new immersive learning spaces and how qualitative research plays out within a number of environmental and cultural variables (Savin-Baden & Howell Major, 2010). The development and use of new technology in learning environments, in which education is delivered and supported through ICT, compel researchers to face a number of challenges concerning the exploration and how to make new spaces of learning transparent and accessible for research.

In order to capture interaction and learning taking place across the different dimensions of context in time and space, Drotner (2013) emphasizes the need for

3

"processual methodologies". In a similar manner, Pink (2012) uses the concept of "the multi-sensory Internet". According to Drotner, online and offline participant observation, video recording, and participatory design – among others – are good examples of processual methodologies already taking place in qualitative research within media studies and education studies. Educational ethnography is a subfield in education research, which has its roots in anthropology and microsociology. From the late 1960s, researchers within this field were mostly studying class and gender in school. However, from the 1990s, the research interest began to widen and became more oriented towards out of school activities – vocational training, learning in community centres, in sport clubs, museums and as part of the entire life course (Drotner, 2013). New perspectives on learning challenge the traditional focus in ethnography on bounded physical places as the centre of interest (Leander et al., 2010). According to Drotner, digital forms of learning change the dilemmas for the researcher utilizing processual methodologies when it comes to defining the research subject or research object, and it changes the relation between the researcher and the research person. In order to understand and capture learning in transaction, Drotner claims it is time to develop multi-sited research designs and new creative forms of data collection. Furthermore, the new blend of physical places and virtual spaces of meaning making in these learning processes demands a multidimensional way of examining and analysing these processes *in situ*, when they play out synchronously online and offline (Drotner, 2013). Current research taking place across a range of times and sites underscores the need to develop new methodological approaches and forms of analysis.

OUTLINE OF THE BOOK

This volume presents researchers who use a wide variety of perspectives and qualitative methods to explore ICT in a number of different learning contexts. The following chapters can be categorized into three main themes: (1) challenges when exploring networked learning and virtual environments; (2) challenges for researcher interaction in various learning sites; and (3) challenges when exploring children's meaning making in digital contexts. The final chapter draws on the former chapters, views the way ahead and suggests some future approaches important for research and methodological considerations when researching learning contexts of the future.

Part I: Challenges When Exploring Networked Learning and Virtual Environments

The three chapters in the first section of this volume discuss challenges when investigating learning across various virtual environments and networked contexts. In chapter two, Murphy, Castillo, Zahra and Wagner explore how learning experiences that are mediated by mobile technologies (mLearning) expand opportunities to assist and support learning and expand the frontier for educational initiatives from different parts of the world. Mobile technologies may allow users to select when, where and how their learning activities occur. Providing innovative opportunities for highly individualized learning pushes the boundaries of traditional educational tools, which were typically confined by content, location and functionality. The authors claim it is of critical importance to define new ways for understanding how learning occurs with mobile technologies and to improve methodological approaches for analysing learning outcomes across multiple online and offline contexts. By suggesting research designs sensitive to the ways in which mobile applications are used in and across distinct settings, Murphy and her colleagues provide a detailed characterization of core elements that contribute to an mLearning design solution and the particular techniques used to promote behavioural change and learning.

In chapter three, Stornaiuolo and Hall address the dual challenge of investigating how ICTs are changing the face of education while also trying to mediate the use of these digital technologies in the research process itself. The authors illustrate how challenges of mobility and interconnectedness in networked communicative contexts are manifested in one of their projects as *resonance*, the intertextual echoing of ideas across spaces, people and texts. To illustrate the concept, they trace one example of resonance across the data by following how conversations around sexuality emerged across the networked community and how this emergence was crystallized in participants' semiotic activity. Stornaiuolo and Hall discuss the persistent challenges in addressing issues of resonance and, indeed, in capturing and representing the complexity of participants' learning and engagement across spaces. They claim that there is a need to weave multiple methodologies together in order to continue expanding researchers' methodological toolkits and enable them to work synergistically across research methodologies. Such an effort across interdisciplinary and technological frontiers is necessary in order to account for the emergent dimensions of meaning making in networked contexts.

In chapter four, Burkle and Magee discuss methodological challenges in designing educational research projects on videogames and 3D online virtual reality environments. The authors explore how research possibilities and challenges are emerging because digital environments and virtual reality are transforming the way learners and instructors interact with each other in and across contexts. Using data from two parallel research projects, the chapter analyses the research challenges of exploring students' self-identity, problem solving, learning motivations and value construction when interacting with each other for learning in a virtual environment. The authors suggest a practical and more straight-forward research approach, such as the think aloud approach that has been used when researchers examine the thought processes of users engaged in technology-mediated environments. Burkle and Magee claim that such an open methodological approach is capable of examining learning in videogames and virtual realities by, for example, letting the research process be guided by questions articulated by the research persons.

Part II: Challenges for Researcher Interaction in Various Learning Sites

The two chapters in the second section of the book discuss challenges and possibilities in the relationship between the researcher and the researched person in digital learning environments. In chapter five, Donovan discusses how participatory research and design with youth co-researchers presents methodological challenges that, when they are met, help build capacities for critiquing and engaging private modes of knowledge production. Donovan claims that the productive and entertaining promises of proprietary communication, education and play media in post-industrial societies have led to the widespread adoption among youth whose daily activities now generate troves of data that are mined for profit. As young people learn to text, email, browse and search within such environments, their identity configurations link up with informational modes of capitalist production. In his chapter, Donovan presents a methodological approach aimed at involving young people in the collaborative process of research and reflection through the co-design of an open source social network.

In chapter six, Hatlevik and Egeberg present and discuss experiences from a research project where researchers were asked to follow the implementation of interactive whiteboards in a school. They discuss the relationship between the researcher and the research person from another angle than the previous chapter, particularly problematizing how researchers can manage both the role of the researcher and the educational expert when the researchers and the teachers have different goals and expectations of the outcome of the researchers' participation in the project. From a research perspective, a fundamental question when technology is introduced in schools is how to gather and analyse data that can shed light on issues related to the implementation and use of technology in teaching. A video clip might be used as a tool for researchers achieving consensus when concluding on empirical findings. However, a teacher might view the clip with another intention, for example, to improve his or her practice. Hatlevik and Egeberg suggest constructing research groups that possess the necessary knowledge and experience to achieve the goals of the study and at the same time meet the expectations of the research subjects.

Part III: Challenges When Exploring Children's Meaning Making in Digital Contexts

The two chapters in the last section of the book discuss challenges when exploring and investigating how young people are making meaning across physical places and virtual spaces. In chapter seven, Pribišev Beleslin addresses challenges when combining different methodological approaches in order to investigate how small children make meaning when they use ICT. In order to discover the richness of young children's stories about digital culture, Pribišev Beleslin makes use of a mosaic approach inspired by the "pedagogy of listening", which is based on relations, encounters and dialogues between co-constructers of meaning making. Pribišev Beleslin presents a methodological approach suggesting researchers listen carefully to the children and access their perspectives and early experiences by combining a mosaic of participatory methods. Such an approach represents a source of many pieces in a puzzle that creates an image of children's worlds, both individual and collective.

In chapter eight, Davidsen and Vanderlinde similarly apply the children's perspective and highlight the importance – as well as the lack – of doing so in studies of ICT. The authors discuss the challenges and potentials of using micro multimodal video analysis of children's collaborative learning activities supported by touch-screen technology. Their research project integrating touch-screens in two primary school classrooms explores children between the age of eight and nine years. As a methodological approach, Davidsen and Vanderlinde suggest making use of micro multimodal video analysis in order to provide thick descriptions of how young children experience and interact with ICT in a specific context, focusing on how they engage in collaboration through language, gestures and digital learning materials. Most importantly, their contributions together with Pribišev Beleslin's chapter show how to conduct research from the children's perspective, and how such a perspective can enrich both teachers' pedagogical thinking as well as qualify our scientific understanding of how children are acting and making meaning in a digital environment.

FINAL CONSIDERATIONS

The ninth and concluding chapter in this volume continues the discussion from the introductory chapter regarding new perspectives and understanding of space as a fluid concept and the challenges investigating learning that takes place across space over time. In this chapter, Gilje and Erstad discuss transitions and trajectories in young peoples' learning lives and in particular the methodological challenges of studying learning across contexts. Technological developments create changes in the social practices we are studying, and provide us with new tools for doing empirical work. Gilje and Erstad's concerns are how we can research the learning lives of young adults. Methodologically, it is complex and difficult to follow learners across and between sites or conceptually, tracing, translating and reconfiguring understanding across contexts. Drawing on two large studies (Learning Lives and KnowMo), the authors suggest how research on trajectories of participation and transitions in young adults' learning lives can take place across contexts. Based on experiences from these projects, the authors raise some issues and challenges about using digital media to collect and analyse data, and ways of involving study subjects as co-researchers.

The overall aim of this volume is to explore some key challenges for educational research in digital contexts. The result is a collection of contributions that do not focus on a particular aspect of qualitative methods, but rather a volume that reflects on both the variety of accessible research methods and possibilities for developing new methods designed to capture new understandings of learning taking place across and between online and offline spaces. The various contributions in this volume explore the three main challenges we claim are raised by the growth of ICT in educational research today. These challenges are (1) how research manages to explore networked learning within a multi-faceted ICT environment; (2) how researchers experience the research context and interact with various actors within these settings; and (3) how children make meaning across physical places and virtual spaces. Together, these nine chapters problematize how we observe and describe emerging forms of learning in current educational research when ICT is both the medium and the object of research.

REFERENCES

Athanassios, J. (2012). *Research on e-learning and ICT in education.* New York, NY: Springer.

Buckingham, D. (2008). *Youth, identity and digital media.* Cambridge, MA: MIT Press.

Drotner, K. (2013). Processual methodologies and digital forms of learning. In O. Erstad & J. Sefton-Green (Eds.), *Identity, community, and learning lives in the digital age* (pp. 39-56). Cambridge: Cambridge University Press.

Erstad, O. (2012). The learning lives of digital youth – Beyond the formal and informal. *Oxford Review of Education, 38*(1), 25-43.

Furlong, J., & Davies, C. (2012). Young people, new technologies and learning at home: Taking context seriously. *Oxford Review of Education, 38*(1), 45-62.

Gee, J. P. (2004). *Situated language and learning: A critique of traditional schooling.* London: Routledge.

Ito, M. (2009). *Engineering play: A cultural history of children's software.* Cambridge, MA: MIT Press.

Ito, M., Gutiérrez, K. D., Livingstone, S., Penuel, B., Rhodes, J., Salen, K., Schor, J., et al. (2013). *Connected learning: An agenda for research and design.* Irvine, CA: Digital Media and Learning Research Hub.

Kalervo, G. N. (2011). *Education policy, space and the city: Markets and the (in)visibility of race.* New York, NY: Routledge.

Laurillard, D. (2012). *Teaching as a design science: Building pedagogical patterns for learning and technology.* New York, NY: Taylor and Francis.

Leander, K. M., Phillips, N. C., & Taylor, K. H. (2010). The changing social spaces of learning: Mapping new mobilities. *Review of Research in Education, 34*(1), 329-394.

Miller, D., & Horst, H. A. (2012). *Digital anthropology.* London: Berg.

Moje, E. B. (2004). Powerful spaces: Tracing the out-of-school literacy spaces of Latino/a youth. In K. Leander & M. Sheehy (Eds.), *Spatializing literacy research and practice* (pp. 15-38). New York, NY: Peter Lang.

Pink, S. (2012). Visual ethnography and the Internet. Visuality, virtuality and the spatial turn. In S. Pink (Ed.), *Advances in visual methodology* (pp. 112-130). London: Sage.

Price, S., Jewitt, C., & Brown, B. (2013a). Introduction. In S. Price, C. Jewitt, & B. Brown (Eds.), *Sage handbook of digital technology research* (pp. 1-5). London: Sage.

Price, S., Jewitt, C., & Brown, B. (2013b). Afterword: Looking to the future. In S. Price, C. Jewitt, & B. Brown (Eds.), *Sage handbook of digital technology research* (pp. 473-475). London: Sage.

Punie, Y., & Ala-Mutka, K. (2007). Future learning spaces: New ways of learning and new digital skills to learn. *Nordic Journal of Digital Literacy, 4*(2), 210-225.

Savin-Baden, M., & Howell Major, C. (2010). *New approaches to qualitative research.* Hoboken: Taylor & Francis.

Sefton-Green, J. (2013). *Mapping digital makers: A review exploring everyday creativity, learning lives and the digital.* Oxford: The Nominet Trust.

Sheehy, M., & Leander, K. M. (2004). Introduction. In K. Leander & M. Sheehy (Eds.), *Spatializing literacy research and practice* (pp. 1-14). New York, NY: Peter Lang.

Soja, E. W. (1996). *Thirdspace: Journeys to Los Angeles and other real-and-imagined places.* Cambridge, MA: Blackwell.

Kristin Beate Vasbø
Department of Teacher Education and School Research
University of Oslo
Norway

Greta Björk Gudmundsdottir
The Norwegian Centre for ICT in Education
Norway

PART I

CHALLENGES WHEN EXPLORING NETWORKED LEARNING AND VIRTUAL ENVIRONMENTS

KATIE M. MURPHY, NATHAN M. CASTILLO, FATIMA T. ZAHRA, AND DANIEL A. WAGNER

2. MOBILE LEARNING DESIGN SOLUTIONS

Innovations in Learning through the Use of Mobiles across Contexts

INTRODUCTION

As the world prepares for the next generation of United Nations development goals, two critical priorities will be needed to build a sustainable global community and economy: advancing educational quality through improved learning experiences and reducing inequities in educational opportunities. Addressing these priorities within diverse contexts across the world presents a formidable challenge that has not yet been achieved despite major investments in school infrastructure, teacher training and the procurement of learning materials (Patrinos & Psacharopoulos, 2011). At the same time, recent studies of early grade reading have found that many children are unable to read a single word in the language of instruction, even after several years of schooling (Gove & Cvelich, 2010). Further, variations in school quality have been found to have a greater influence on educational outcomes and economic growth than the number of years of schooling (Hanushek & Woesman, 2007). As these studies underscore, increased enrolment and years of schooling are not a panacea for the learning failures observed throughout the world. While there is a strong case for the inadequacy and inefficient distribution of current educational funding (UNESCO, 2013a), improved development investments must build upon effective strategies and draw from innovative solutions to boost learning opportunities, in schools as well as out-of-school.

New information and communications technologies (ICTs) offer hope in contexts where past interventions have been unsuccessful and in locations where populations have been marginalized or excluded from social services, schools or learning resources. This is particularly the case with mLearning, or learning experiences that are mediated by mobile technologies (Winters, 2006). MLearning allow users to have the opportunity to engage in learning processes at any time, at any place, and in an individualized manner (Quinn, 2001; Peters, 2007). Mobile technologies include a broad range of portable electronic devices such as: laptop and hand-held computers, tablets, cellular phones, personal media players, among others. By virtue of being portable, increasingly accessible, affordable and ubiquitous (UNESCO, 2013b), mobile devices may provide opportunities for

G.B. Gudmundsdottir and K.B. Vasbø (Eds.), Methodological Challenges When Exploring Digital Learning Spaces in Education, 13–27.

improved learning experiences across a wide array of contexts including the schools, neighbourhoods and homes with children and adults that have been traditionally marginalized (Muyinda, Lubega, & Lynch, 2010).

The use of mobile technologies as a learning tool has expanded beyond high-income settings, and is now becoming prevalent in low-income contexts in developing countries (Nugroho & Lonsdale, 2010; Hinostroza, Isaacs & Bougroum, 2012; Wagner, 2013). Similarly, mobile technologies have been used in agriculture, banking, health and other sectors throughout the world. While early applications have primarily focused on data collection and information transmission, they have also been used to promote behaviour change aimed at improving economic, physical and social wellbeing (e.g. Fjeldsoe, Marshall, & Miller, 2009; Cole-Lewis, & Kershaw, 2010; Cole & Fernando, 2012; Free et al., 2013).

Apart from the potential to increase access to information and learning activities, mobile technologies can include interactive and multi-functional capabilities that differentiate mLearning from learning processes that typically occur using other types of educational tools. For instance, traditional textbooks may be considered *mobile* tools in that they often are designed to be portable resources for classroom-based coursework and at-home study. Yet traditional text books face several challenges in the context of low-resource settings and developing countries: they are limited to a finite amount of information and educational activities contained within the text, which take substantial amount of time and resources to revise and update; they are often expensive to produce and distribute; they are printed in the languages determined by the government or educational publisher, usually based on political and economic factors; they are prone to damage and destruction; and their ability to serve as an effective learning tool often hinges on the instructor's training and familiarity of the specific text (Glewwe, Hanushek, Humpage, & Ravina, 2011; Lockheed & Hanushek, 1988).

Mobile technologies do not have immunity to these challenges, yet innovative designs can address many of the issues related to content limitations, cost, distribution, language and durability. Furthermore, within one device, mobile technologies can enable information access, communication, social exchange, participation in interactive games, location and geographic navigation services and other functions that are not typical characteristics of a single educational tool. Unlike conventional learning tools designed for specific functions and contexts, mobile technologies may allow users to select *when, where* and *how* their learning activities occur, providing innovative opportunities for highly individualized learning (Peters, 2007).

The potential for multi-functional and individualized learning through mLearning applications pushes the boundaries of traditional educational tools, which were typically confined by content, location and functionality. It is therefore of critical importance to define new ways for understanding how learning occurs with mobile technologies and to improve methods for analysing learning outcomes. This requires a careful examination of the various aspects of an mLearning initiative that influences *how, where* and *why* applications are used, as well as an

14

understanding of the human interactions that occur during and after use and the changes in human behaviour and learning that result.

Several scholars have proposed conceptual frameworks for understanding mLearning applications (e.g., Motiwalla, 2007; Park, 2011; Muyinda, Lubega, Lynch, & Van der Weide, 2011), employing various combinations of technological, pedagogical and contextual factors. In formulating a multi-dimensional framework for mLearning, Muyinda and colleagues (2011) provide a useful comparison of several relevant frameworks, highlighting existing research gaps, such as the lack of consideration for device limitations, network conditions, pedagogical approaches, user characteristics, costs, supportive policy frameworks and variations in learning content sources. Despite the recent scholarship in the field of mLearning, each proposed framework falls short in providing clear guidance for mLearning research methodology.

Addressing the need for a versatile mLearning framework to guide research methodology, the present chapter draws from past research and offers a basic conceptual framework that builds from a recent landscape research review of mobile technology for reading (Wagner, 2013). In the proposed framework, key attributes and variables that contribute to the *design solution* are identified and described. Throughout the following three sections, the term *design solution* refers to a complex composition of factors that contribute to an mLearning initiative. The first section highlights three key elements that influence an mLearning design: purposes, devices and users; the second section describes the way in which contexts and the user's environment interacts with mLearning processes; while the third section focuses on the need to identify and evaluate specific learning techniques employed within the mLearning design solution. Throughout, a number of methodological considerations for mLearning research are discussed.

The key components described below contribute to the basic structure of the proposed conceptual framework for mLearning design solutions. This framework can provide guidance for improved research methodology that investigates specific components of mLearning applications, their interactions with other components of the design solution and variations in outcomes and effects as a result of such interactions. Applied to research and evaluation studies, the design solution framework may advance understanding of learning processes through mobile devices, paving the way for improved evidence-based design of future innovations.

A CONCEPTUAL FRAMEWORK FOR MLEARNING:
PURPOSES, DEVICES AND USERS

The complex factors that contribute to the design process of mLearning initiatives have not been adequately understood through existing methodological approaches. In the practical application of any mLearning initiative, the design process is embedded in contextual conditions that include cultural, economic, political and social influences. The dynamic interactions among these factors contribute to the contextual ecosystem of mLearning. Within this ecosystem, three key components form the basic structure of a comprehensive mLearning design and evaluation strategy: (a) intervention purposes; (b) device specifications; and (c) end-user characteristics (for a more detailed discussion, see Wagner, 2013). Located at the intersection of these three factors, one or more design solutions may emerge to encompass the appropriate content and implementation strategy of an mLearning initiative, as depicted in Figure 1. A brief description of each component highlights key variables that impact the formative processes of mLearning design, which should be considered when developing appropriate research methodologies.

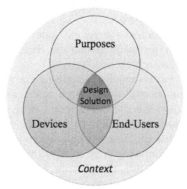

Figure 1. Design solution at the intersection of devices, end-users and purposes

(a) How Does the "Purpose" of the Intervention Shape Design?

The design of mLearning initiatives often stem from the identification of a problem, gap or need, which may be conceptualized as the intervention purpose. Intervention purposes are sometimes explicitly stated by program designers, while at other times can only be implied from program reports or project websites. As described in Wagner (2013), primary intervention purposes include:

– *Formal learning and instruction*: drawing from structured, instructor-led pedagogical methods that typically form part of an established program of study.
– *Informal learning:* focusing on less structured, user-centred pedagogical methods.
– *Content delivery:* providing users with information, textbooks, curricular resources and reading materials, without explicitly engaging in interactive activities.
– *Training:* supporting professional skill development for adults or facilitators who serve as intermediaries for other learners.
– *Data collection and assessment*: using mobile technologies for monitoring, evaluation and learning assessments.
– *Communication*: providing increased opportunities for social interaction and communication among target users.

Many interventions do not fall exclusively within a single purpose and may combine two or more purposes within a single initiative. Yet in each mLearning initiative, the clear identification of the purpose provides a roadmap for the selection of research questions and outcome indicators that are essential in the methodological design of an mLearning evaluation. For example, in comparing initiatives designed for similar purposes, field testing, randomized control trials and quasi-experimental studies can be used to investigate differences in learning outcomes and student experiences in mLearning compared to non-mLearning approaches. Observational studies and ethnographic techniques could offer insight into the ways in which learners respond to the use of mLearning for various purposes. Additionally, the analysis of activity logs from mLearning applications can be used to better understand if the design solution achieves the intended purpose, or if users have found various ways to re-purpose an mLearning application.

(b) How Do the Specifications of Particular Devices Shape Design?

Mobile technologies encompass a broad variation of functionality, cost, accessibility and connectivity and these attributes have a direct impact on mLearning design solutions. Commonly used mobile devices include laptops, tablets, portable media players and phones that range from basic voice and text message capability to advanced or smartphones that mimic some of the capabilities of computers or tablets. Interventions that make use of such devices are expanding in high and middle-income countries; yet economic, logistical and practical considerations can often weaken the case for mLearning in low-income countries (GSMA, 2010). Challenges to mLearning sustainability are common in education systems with limited resources, as issues related to device procurement, appropriate technology use, connectivity, device maintenance and repair often threaten the development of viable implementation strategies. Nonetheless, recent funding efforts that promote innovation are encouraging increased experimentation with mobile solutions among organizations (Hinostroza et al., 2012), and may address some of the current challenges of mLearning in developing contexts.

The particular specifications of a device influence the developers' ability to include interactive activities, audio and video content, or e-books that require large amounts of memory. Similarly, certain devices may be less appropriate for particular environmental, infrastructural or social conditions (e.g., places that may be prone to extremes in temperature or weather, may not have adequate power supply or repair facilities to maintain device operation, or may be sold or stolen). At the same time, an overreliance on device design limits resources for capacity development and maintenance (DeBoer, 2009), and such oversight can ultimately impact the long-term usage and the learning outcomes of an otherwise innovative intervention.

Device specifications, including user interface, procurement costs, connectivity, multi-media functionality, durability, maintenance and repair issues are critical considerations for mLearning research. The analysis of device specifications is a critical step in formative research and process evaluation, as it may be used to select the most appropriate device for a particular context, which requires field testing, costing studies and the analysis of user interaction with potential devices.

(c) How Do the Characteristics of the End-User Shape Design?

Intervention design strategies must take into serious consideration the specific characteristics of the intended end-user population. These include: age, location, socio-economic status (SES), education and literacy level, language, culture, gender, health profiles and individual learning differences. Further, individuals' learning dispositions and their different types of knowledge relevant to the mLearning application also influence the design strategy (Mishra & Koehler, 2006). An understanding of the learner's characteristics and baseline knowledge can inform the design of instructional content and support materials, taking advantage of observed strengths and compensating for weaknesses or knowledge gaps. In this sense, a comprehensive mLearning design should complement end-user characteristics.

In order to respond to end-user characteristics and variations in learning dispositions, teachers and instructional materials need to adapt pedagogical approaches when using mLearning technologies. For example, a study examining Bangladesh Virtual Interactive classrooms (BVIC), the largest distance education project by the Bangladesh Open University, found that significant changes in content and pedagogical approaches were needed to appropriately respond to end-user characteristics and learning dispositions toward the interactive learning management system and SMS-based lessons (Islam, Ashraf, Rahman, & Rahman, 2005; Grönlund & Islam, 2010). Similarly, in a study conducted by Nihuka and Voogt (2011) for the Open University of Tanzania, the role of teachers and their attitudes toward various types of technologies was identified as an important influence on the end-user's learning experience.

With a comprehensive understanding of the end-user characteristics, learning dispositions and appropriate pedagogy, mLearning applications hold great potential for educational initiatives specifically tailored to distinct populations of learners. For example, mLearning applications in high-income countries suggest that the use of mobile technologies can assist in language and communication development for children with Autism Spectrum Disorder by allowing learners to manipulate and combine graphic representations of words and concepts (Shane et al., 2011). In low and middle income countries, there are several examples of mLearning applications that have been designed to address specific needs of particular demographic groups, such as women, ethno-linguistic minorities, or out of school youth (e.g. Kumar, Reddy, Tewari, Agrawal, & Kam, 2012; Vosloo, Walton, & Deumert, 2009; Zain, Mahmud, & Hassan, 2013).

Despite the great potential to tailor mLearning initiatives to distinct user characteristics for individualized learning experiences, this also raises important concerns that are serious considerations for research methodology. User demographics and trends and patterns in personal usage of mLearning applications, such as the amount of time per day a user interacts with a mobile device, provide valuable data for the analysis of mLearning applications. Yet research approaches that take advantage of user information from mobile technology require careful consideration of privacy and ethics. Unauthorized disclosures or inappropriate use of personal information and location data could lead to embarrassment, marginalization or threaten rights to privacy and safety. In the absence of established, universal standards for mobile data use and analysis, researchers and practitioners should exert substantial attention to these important ethical issues relevant to mLearning.

MULTIPLE CONTEXTS OF MLEARNING

The key components of mLearning design: purposes, devices and end-users must be analysed through the lens of dynamic, multiple contexts in order to gain a more comprehensive understanding of how these initiatives function in the real world, within and across distinct contexts. For example, learning processes that are prompted through the use of a mobile phone-based language learning application cannot be adequately studied in a controlled classroom or laboratory setting. Instead, research designs must be sensitive to the ways in which mobile applications are used in and across distinct settings. In this sense, mLearning contrasts with conventional learning interventions, whether part of a formal curriculum or an out-of-school educational program, which are often designed to fit within the circumstances and conditions of a particular context. Variations in these conditions can be conceptualized as part of a continuum, ranging from formal to non-formal learning contexts, as illustrated in Figure 2 (see also Wagner, Murphy, & de Korne, 2012).

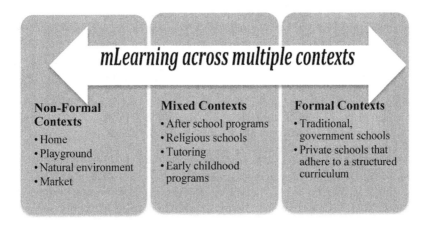

Figure 2. Multiple contexts of mLearning

Formal and Non-Formal Contexts

The traditional Western classroom typifies the formal learning context and is a model that has been replicated in schools and learning institutions throughout the world. School directors, ministers of education and most international agencies tend to focus resources on improving learning within these formal learning contexts, as they are spaces that are specifically designed for educational purposes and may be monitored and controlled. On the other end of the spectrum are spaces that have not been consciously designed for educational purposes, yet where learning still occurs, which can be described as non-formal contexts. These may include the natural environment, homes, markets and neighbourhoods, among others. After-school education programs, preschools, non-traditional or independent schools, educational drop-in centres and a broad variety of other initiatives fall on varying points along the two ends of the learning contexts spectrum. The approach adopted by many conventional learning initiatives has been to determine a design strategy based on a defined *use case* that is grounded in a specific context (e.g., Henry, 2001). Classroom-based science experiments, after-school youth literacy programs, desktop computer games to improve math or typing, offer a few examples of learning initiatives designed for specific contexts. Learning applications on mobile devices, in contrast, typically operate in multiple contexts and warrant a distinct approach to design and research methodology (Park, 2011).

Mobiles and Learning Innovations in Multiple Contexts

The 'm' in mLearning distinguishes it from other learning media precisely because its applications are mobile and it is difficult to confine use to one particular context. Although some projects may try to restrict the use of an mLearning application to classrooms or after-school settings, one of the unique advantages of mLearning is its ability to adapt and integrate across contexts, as mLearning becomes increasingly ubiquitous (Park, 2011; Shuler, 2009; Peters, 2007). This conceptualization of mLearning encompasses dynamic transitions across time and space, as well as enhanced opportunities for the spontaneous creation of virtual contexts formed through social interaction among learners around a shared conversation or topic of interest (Sharples, Taylor, & Vavoula, 2007). Capturing and describing the influence of the diverse and reciprocal contexts on mLearning activities represents a challenge in the field of educational research.

Furthermore, as technology advances, mobile devices will likely improve their ability to sense and detect contextual cues relevant to the user in a particular time and space to create highly adaptable learning applications, as illustrated by advancements in Context-Aware Mobile Learning (Tan, Liu, & Burkle, 2013). To better understand the complex ways in which learners interact within mobile contexts, traditional methods of observation or self-reported surveys may be used, and the location-tracking and usage-monitoring capacities within mobile devices may also be employed to gain a more comprehensive understanding of specific learning activities that occur in various contexts.

MLEARNING TECHNIQUES WITHIN THE DESIGN SOLUTION

The analysis of any mLearning initiative requires a consideration of the intended purpose, the advantages and disadvantages of the selected device or devices, the capabilities and needs of the end-user population, together with an understanding of user interactions across multiple contexts. At the same time, mode of delivery (e.g., synchronous or asynchronous, group or individual use, etc.), the intensity and duration of the intervention, the characteristics of those involved in the design and implementation (including the level of participation of end-users in the process), and the pedagogical approach and use of specific learning techniques all have a direct influence on the overall *design solution*. Expanding on the conceptual framework presented earlier, Figure 3 includes some of the key factors within each component, including the important considerations that influence the design solution.

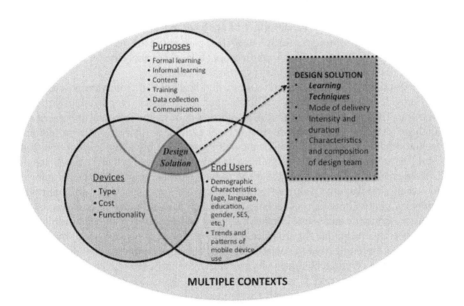

Figure 3. Detailed description of design solution components

21

The highlighted *learning techniques* represent a critical piece of the design solution with a direct bearing on our understanding of the interaction between human learning and mobile technology. Learning techniques are specific applications of theory-grounded strategies used to prompt the acquisition of new knowledge, skills and behaviour change. The concept of learning technique analysis borrows from recent work in the field of behaviour change, public health and more recently mHealth (Abraham & Michie, 2008; Free et al., 2013). This approach recognizes the need for methodological designs that not only measure longer-term outcomes (e.g., educational gains), but that also investigate various techniques that may be used to promote learning, social interaction and behaviour change. The clear identification and analysis of specific learning techniques allows for an improved understanding of effective strategies that can be used to inform future mLearning initiatives.

In the field of public health, Abraham and Michie (2008) proposed the need for a clearly defined taxonomy of behaviour change techniques based on prominent learning and behaviour change theories in public health interventions (cf. Glanz, Rimer, & Viswanath, 2008). Drawing from this work, the analysis of mLearning techniques can provide important insights regarding the ways in which particular interventions function. Table 1 provides some examples of mLearning techniques, how each technique may be applied in an mLearning initiative, and relevant research topics that may be designed to analyse and measure discrete aspects of each mLearning technique. Such research topics could be incorporated into the methodological design through observational studies, analysis of activity logs, randomized control trials and quasi-experimental studies.

Descriptions of mLearning initiatives often highlight the intervention purposes, but provide scant descriptions of the actual mechanisms employed to promote learning. This oversight hampers the advancement of methodological approaches to analyse, evaluate and compare distinct mLearning initiatives. The mLearning techniques listed in Table 1 provide a small sample of a broad range of options that could be considered when designing a learning strategy. Further research would offer increased understanding about the varieties of learning techniques employed by each innovation. Targeted research would also provide an improved understanding of how various techniques function across a range of contexts, as the cultural, economic and social climate may play an important role in determining the most effective technique for a particular context. For example, are social modelling techniques more effective in socially oriented societies compared to individualistic societies? Are certain techniques more effective for particular age groups? What are the device characteristics and implementation strategies required for various techniques? By identifying which techniques or combination of techniques are at play in a mobile application, researchers may better understand effective approaches to promote increased learning and achieve educational goals.

Table 1. Useful mLearning techniques drawn from Abraham and Michie's (2008) taxonomy of behaviour change for public health

mLearning Techniques	Example Uses of mLearning Techniques	Examples of Relevant Research Topics
Strength and Barrier Identification	Prompt identification of knowledge areas or skills that serve as personal strengths, as well as skills and abilities that could be improved	Self-awareness of knowledge areas or skills that serve as personal assets as well as learning "barriers"
Contingent rewards	Provide positive reinforcement for completed tasks; reward values may increase with task difficulty	User response and changes in motivation resulting from positive reinforcement and rewards
Encouragement	Provide motivational support without rewards, and that is not contingent upon the completion of tasks	User response and changes in motivation resulting from encouragement and support
Graded tasks	Introduce simple tasks, increase difficulty, provide hints or help until task is performed. Continue to increase difficulty until learning objective is met	Analysis of task performance, persistence towards a defined learning objective
Performance feedback	Provide immediate or short-term feedback on performance of a specific task or learning objective, to compare with set standards or goals	User response to feedback, analysis of task performance
Self-established goal setting	Prompt intention formation or goal setting with specific targets	User response to feedback, analysis of task performance
Social comparison	Provide information about peers' behaviours or others' attitude toward the behaviour	User response to others' behaviours and/or knowledge of the others' attitudes about behaviours
Social modelling	Allow users to observe others performing or demonstrating task and completing set goal; encourage imitation of task	Task performance before and after observations of social modelling

CONCLUSION

The expansion of mobile technology for learning presents new opportunities to address persistent challenges to achieving improved and equitable learning experiences – even in some of the most marginalized contexts of developing countries. At the same time, a major impediment to progress in this field has been the lack of clarity surrounding the notion of mLearning. The conceptual framework proposed in this chapter attempts to provide a detailed characterization of the key components that contribute to an mLearning design solution and the particular techniques used to promote behavioural change and learning. The application of this framework can provide a more comprehensive understanding of an intervention's impact as well as promote the appropriate adoption, adaptation and replication of future mLearning innovations.

Several important considerations are central in the development of an appropriate research or evaluation strategy. Among the most pertinent of these considerations include issues of privacy and ethics in the use of personal information, and the need to support the integration of local expertise in research design and implementation. The possibility of tracking learning activities across various contexts could provide important insights not only for mLearning, but also for education and learning initiatives more broadly. With an improved understanding of how and where students engage in mLearning, educators, parents, caregivers, policymakers and others may effectively identify key opportunities for new interventions to augment positive learning behaviours. At the same time, mLearning methodologies that make use of user data must also be sensitive to ethical responsibilities to protect personal information and privacy, particularly in contexts where protective legal structures and policies are absent or weak.

With a large majority of the world's population living in low and middle-income countries, greater efforts should also be focused on ways in which mLearning may operate in places where the cultural, economic, environmental and social climate differs from highly industrialized nations. An understanding of these ecological factors requires insights and expertise from local researchers, community members and the targeted end-users. Mlearning can provide an extended platform for research, monitoring and continuous innovation by local researchers, as they can use real-time data to better understand users behaviour and experiences with devices. Also, research designs should be sensitive to populations that are often excluded from mainstream education programs in low-resource settings, such as women, ethnic and linguistic minorities and learners with physical and cognitive disabilities. Often subjects of marginalization and exclusion, these populations may have the greatest gains from new applications of mLearning initiatives that may be adapted to particular learning needs across a range of contexts.

Looking forward, mLearning specialists will continue to explore new ways to harness the multi-functional capabilities of mobile technologies. Concomitant methodological approaches will be needed to better understand how learning occurs with mobile devices in and across multiple contexts. There is little doubt that future mLearning designs will require new thinking that expands, extends and interconnects the traditional boundaries of education, learning and technology.

REFERENCES

Abraham, C., & Michie, S. (2008). A taxonomy of behaviour change techniques used in interventions. *Health Psychology, 27*(3), 379-387.

Cole, S., & Fernando, A. (2012, November). *The value of advice: Evidence from mobile phone-based agricultural extension.* Harvard Business School Finance Working Paper No. 13-047. Retrieved from http://papers.ssrn.com/sol3/papers.cfm?abstract_id=2179008

Cole-Lewis, H., & Kershaw, T. (2010). Text messaging as a tool for behaviour change in disease prevention and management. *Epidemiologic Reviews, 32*(1), 56-69.

DeBoer, J. (2009). The relationship between environmental factors and usage behaviours at 'Hole-in-the-wall' computers. *International Journal of Educational Development, 29*, 91-98.

Fjeldsoe, B. S., Marshall, A. L., & Miller, Y. D. (2009). Behaviour change interventions delivered by mobile telephone short-message service. *American Journal of Preventive Medicine, 36*(2), 165-173.

Free C., Phillips G., Watson, Galli, L., Felix L., et al. (2013). The effectiveness of mobile-health technology-based health behaviour change or disease management interventions for health care consumers: A systematic review. *PLoS Med 10*(1), e1001362. Retrieved from http://www.researchgate.net/publication/235371977_The_effectiveness_of_mobile-health_technology-based_health_behaviour_change_or_disease_management_interventions_for_health_care_consumers_a_systematic_review

Glanz, K., Rimer, B. K., & Viswanath, K. (2008). *Health behavior and health education: Theory, research, and practice.* San Francisco, CA: John Wiley & Sons.

Glewwe, P. W., Hanushek, E. A., Humpage, S. D., & Ravina, R. (2011). *School resources and educational outcomes in developing countries: A review of the literature from 1990 to 2010.* NBER Working Paper No. 17554. Cambridge, MA: National Bureau of Economic Research. Retrieved from http://www.nber.org/papers/w17554

Gove, A., & Cvelich, P. (2010). *Early reading: Igniting education for all.* A report by the Early Grade Learning Community of Practice. Washington, DC: RTI.

Grönlund, Å., & Islam, Y. M. (2010). A mobile e-Learning environment for developing countries: The Bangladesh virtual interactive classroom. *Information Technology for Development, 16*(4), 244-259.

GSMA. (2010). *mLearning: A platform for educational opportunities at the base of the pyramid.* GSMA. Retrieved from http://www.mobileactive.org/files/file_uploads/mLearning_Report_Final_Dec2010.pdf

Hanushek, E. A., & Woessmann, L. (2007). *The role of education quality for economic growth.* Policy Research Working Paper Series 4122. Washington, DC: World Bank.

Henry, P. (2001). E-learning technology, content and services. *Education & Training, 43*(4/5), 249-255.

Hinostroza, J. E., Isaacs, S., & Bougroum, M. (2012). *Information and communications technologies for improving students' learning opportunities and outcomes in developing countries.* Brookings GCL draft report. Washington, DC: Brookings Institute.

Islam, Y. M., Ashraf, M., Rahman, Z., & Rahman, M. (2005, May). Mobile technology as a distance learning tool. In *Proceedings of the Seventh International Conference on Enterprise Information Systems*, Miami, U.S. (pp. 226-232).

Kumar, A., Reddy, P., Tewari, A., Agrawal, R., & Kam, M. (2012, May). Improving literacy in developing countries using speech recognition-supported games on mobile devices. In *Proceedings of ACM Conference on Human Factors in Computing Systems (CHI '12)*, Austin, Texas. Retrieved from http://www.cs.cmu.edu/~anujk1/CHI2012b.pdf

Lockheed, M. E., & Hanushek, E. (1988). Improving educational efficiency in developing countries: What do we know? *Compare, 18*(1), 21-38.

Mishra, P., & Koehler, M. (2006). Technological pedagogical content knowledge: A framework for teacher knowledge. *The Teachers College Record, 108*(6), 1017-1054.

Motiwalla, L. F. (2007). Mobile learning: A framework and evaluation. *Computers & Education, 49*(3), 581-596.

Muyinda, P. B., Lubega, J. T., & Lynch, K. (2010). Unleashing mobile phones for research supervision support at Makerere University, Uganda: the lessons learned. *International Journal of Innovation and Learning, 7*(1), 14-34.

Muyinda, P. B., Lubega, J. T., Lynch, K., & van der Weide, T. (2011). A framework for instantiating pedagogic mlearning objects applications. In A. Cerone & P. Pihlajasaari (Eds.), *Theoretical aspects of computing-ICTAC 2011* (pp. 194-217). Springer-Verlag: Berlin Heidelberg,

Nihuka, K. A., & Voogt, J. (2011). Instructors and students competences, perceptions and access to e-learning technologies: Implications for e-learning implementation at the Open University of Tanzania. *International Journal on E-Learning, 10*(1), 63-85.

Nugroho, D., & Lonsdale, M. (2010). *Evaluation of OLPC programs globally: A literature review.* Version 4. Canberra: ACER. Retrieved from
http://wiki.laptop.org/images/a/a5/OLPC_Lit_Review_v4_Aug2010.pdf

Park, Y. (2011). A pedagogical framework for mobile learning: Categorizing educational applications of mobile technologies into four types. *The International Review of Research in Open and Distance Learning, 12*(2), 78-102.

Patrinos, H. A., & Psacharopoulos, G. (2011). *Education: Past, present and future global challenges.* Washington, DC: World Bank. Retrieved from
https://openknowledge.worldbank.org/handle/10986/3383

Peters, K. (2007). m-Learning: Positioning educators for a mobile, connected future. *International Journal of Research in Open and Distance Learning, 8*(2), 1-17.

Quinn, C. (2001). Get ready for m-learning. *Training and Development, 20* (2), 20-21.

Shane, H. C., Laubscher, E. H., Schlosser, R. W., Flynn, S., Sorce, J. F., & Abramson, J. (2012). Applying technology to visually support language and communication in individuals with autism spectrum disorders. *Journal of Autism and Developmental Disorders, 42*(6), 1228-1235.

Sharples, M., Taylor, J., & Vavoula, G. (2007) A theory of learning for the mobile age. In R. Andrews and C. Haythornthwaite (Eds.), *The Sage Handbook of E-learning Research* (pp. 221-47). London: Sage.

Shuler, C. (2009). *Pockets of potential: Using mobile technologies to promote children's learning.* New York, NY: The Joan Ganz Cooney Center at Sesame Workshop.

Tan, Q., Liu, T. C., & Burkle, M. (2013). Location-based environments for formal and informal learning: Context-aware mobile learning. In D. G. Sampson, P. Isaias, D. Ifenthaler, & J. M. Spector (Eds.), *Ubiquitous and mobile learning in the digital age* (pp. 115-136). New York, NY: Springer.

UNESCO (2013a). *Education for all is affordable – by 2015 and beyond.* EFA Global Monitoring Report. Paris: UNESCO Publishing. Retrieved from
http://unesdoc.unesco.org/images/0021/002199/219998E.pdf

UNESCO (2013b). *Policy guidelines for mobile learning.* Paris: UNESCO Publishing. Retrieved from
http://unesdoc.unesco.org/images/0021/002196/219641E.pdf

Vosloo, S., Walton, M., & Deumert, A. (2009). *m4Lit: A teen m-novel project in South Africa.* Presented at the 8th World Conference on Mobile and Contextual Learning in Orlando, FL. Retrieved from
http://marionwalton.files.wordpress.com/2009/09/mlearn2009_07_sv_mw_ad.pdf

Wagner, D. A. (2013). *M4R: A landscape research review of mobiles for reading.* Philadelphia: International Literacy Institute, University of Pennsylvania.

Wagner, D. A., Murphy, K. M. & de Korne, H. (2012). *Learning first: A research agenda for improving learning in low-income countries.* Center for Universal Education Working Paper. Washington, DC: Brookings Institution.

Winters, N. (2006). What is mobile learning? In M. Sharples (Ed.), *Big issues in mobile learning: Report of a workshop by the kaleidoscope network of excellence mobile learning initiative.* University of Nottingham. Retrieved from http://matchsz.inf.elte.hu/tt/docs/Sharples-20062.pdf

Zain, N. Z. M., Mahmud, M., & Hassan, A. (2013, March). *Utilization of mobile apps among student with learning disability from Islamic perspective.* Paper presented at the 5th International Conference on Information and Communication Technology for the Muslim World (ICT4M), 2013, IEEE, Rabat, Marocco. Retrieved from
http://ieeexplore.ieee.org/xpl/articleDetails.jsp?arnumber=6518889

Katie M. Murphy
Graduate School of Education
University of Pennsylvania
USA

Nathan M. Castillo
Graduate School of Education
University of Pennsylvania
USA

Fatima T. Zahra
Graduate School of Education
University of Pennsylvania
USA

Daniel A. Wagner
Graduate School of Education
University of Pennsylvania
USA

AMY STORNAIUOLO AND MATTHEW HALL

3. TRACING RESONANCE

Qualitative Research in a Networked World

INTRODUCTION

As social networks, mobile devices, and other information and communication technologies (ICTs) increasingly transform educational spaces, researchers are confronted with the dual challenge of investigating how these tools are changing the face of education while also trying to mediate the use of these tools in the research process itself. This chapter focuses on how issues of interconnectivity and mobility are impacting learning spaces and shifting how we engage in qualitative research. The interconnection of people, ideas, modes, and spaces in combination with the increasingly flexible and mobile ways technologies are being taken up by users challenges researchers to develop multifaceted methods for capturing and making sense of these connections and movements.

We begin this chapter by highlighting some of the central challenges facing educational researchers studying networked activities and how scholars have responded by suggesting the expansion of our methodological toolkits (e.g., Baym & Markham, 2009; Beneito-Montagut, 2011; White, 2009). In the following section, we describe our attempts to address these challenges in our work with adolescents and teachers participating in an international, educational social networking project. We illustrate how these challenges of mobility and interconnectedness in networked communicative contexts manifested in our project as resonance (cf. Hull, Stornaiuolo, & Sterponi, 2013), the intertextual echoing of ideas across spaces, people, and texts. We trace one example of resonance across our data, following how conversations around sexuality emerged across the networked community and how this emergence was crystallized in participants' semiotic activity. In the concluding section, we point to persistent challenges in addressing issues of resonance and, indeed, in capturing and representing the complexity of participants' learning and engagement across spaces. We conclude that while it remains important to continue expanding our methodological toolkits across interdisciplinary and technological frontiers, we must also work synergistically across research methodologies in order to account for the emergent dimensions of meaning making in networked contexts.

G.B. Gudmundsdottir and K.B. Vasbø (Eds.), Methodological Challenges When Exploring Digital Learning Spaces in Education, 29–43.

CHALLENGES OF STUDYING NETWORKED LEARNING

As educational researchers explore the ways that digital technologies are intertwined with people's connected learning (Ito et al., 2013), researchers bear increased responsibilities to develop complex methodologies that can move and shift with people as they participate in multifaceted productive practices across a variety of interconnected digital and physical spaces (cf. Madden, Lenhart, Duggan, Cortesi, & Gasser, 2013). Yet in studying the complexities of how people learn and communicate in networked spaces, researchers face significant challenges related to the features of networked publics (Stornaiuolo, Higgs, & Hull, 2013). These features of persistence, replicability, searchability, and scalability have shifted the way we interact online (boyd, 2011), and researchers have called for expanded methodologies to address challenges wrought by these shifts (e.g., Beneito-Montagut, 2011). While scholars sometimes frame these expansions to be new methodological innovations, these extended toolkits often involve importing methods from other disciplines (Wiles, Crow, & Pain, 2011) or using new technologies in our research designs (e.g., Asselin & Moayeri, 2010; White, 2009). In this section we document what we consider three of the most prevalent concerns in conducting research in networked spaces as well as researchers' suggestions to address those challenges.

One of the most well documented shifts in how we conduct research now involves the way we live our lives and make meaning across online and offline spaces, which necessarily complicates what we define as the "site" of our research (Leander & McKim, 2003). In an increasingly connected world that is facilitated by technological and physical links between individuals, spaces, times, and texts, classic understandings of what constitutes a research field site are being complicated (Gupta & Ferguson, 1997), with researchers calling for conceptual frameworks like connective (Leander, 2009) or multi-sited (Marcus, 1995) ethnography to redefine the settings (and boundaries) of research (e.g., Bagley, 2009; Gallagher & Freeman, 2011). For example, Dirksen, Huizing, and Smit (2010) describe how their connective ethnography of a Dutch IT company required them to move beyond physically bounded, local events or places to study practices across face-to-face and digital modes of connection. By tracing the ways that participants created and interacted within a virtual community emerging across on and offline spaces, the authors constructed their "field sites" through a complex methodological network of log file data, interviews, participant observation, documents, and other relevant "spaces" and engagements over time. The multitude of physical locations where the network can be accessed as well as the offline spaces that provide context for interaction on the network adds an expansive layer of data for analysis. As people participate in networked contexts, it has become exceedingly clear that studying one context alone will not suffice if we hope to capture and represent 21st century lived experiences (Pierides, 2010), and our methodological toolkits must therefore be as multifaceted and mobile as the phenomena under consideration.

This expansion of sites and timescales for our research leads to a second major methodological challenge: negotiating the multiplicity of data available. Not only is more data available than ever before, including log file, screen capture, eye tracking, and mapping tools that require more multidimensional data collection and analysis protocols, but this data is available across longer and more complex timescales (Lemke, 2000) and requires us, as Soep (2011) argues, to account methodologically for the "digital afterlife" of participant created artifacts. Researchers must take into account this multiplicity of data across different contexts and over time, a challenge that also carries great potential for developing layered understandings of the complexities of people's meaning making engagements across multiple lived spaces. For example, different forms of log file data offer new windows into online participation, illuminating "lurker" and other less-visible participant roles and opening new avenues for multimodal analyses and visual display (e.g., Dirksen et al., 2010). Given multiple platforms of access, data generated by networked participation can be massive in scale and offer new challenges in managing such "big data", including questions of access to and use of such networked information (boyd & Crawford, 2011).

This rethinking of the contexts and tools for our research is intertwined with ethical entailments of conducting research with digital technologies in networked contexts. One of the most visible problems is how to situate oneself as a researcher in relation to others. The question of what constitutes a public space is still being negotiated—should researchers be able to observe online communities and digital interactions in the "public" domain? Concepts of public and private spaces and texts are contested, and researchers face ethical decisions about how to situate themselves within these spaces. Questions about protecting participants' anonymity grow when material is more easily searchable and identifiable, especially in regard to media that can be quickly distributed to multiple networks beyond the intended audience (Tilley & Woodthorpe, 2011). Whereas the scope and impact of researchers' work used to be fairly narrow, expanded audiences make researchers more accountable to participants and to a broader swath of the public. Networked contexts also add new complexities to persistent questions about the rights of researchers to represent others' experiences (White, 2009), especially when researchers are both members of online communities as well as researchers in these spaces (e.g., Black, 2008). The task of the researcher now is to negotiate access to diverse sites and people across multiple digital and physical spaces and to position oneself in these spaces and in relation to others thoughtfully and ethically.

CHALLENGES IN ACTION: THE SPACE2CRE8 PROJECT

We have experienced these challenges in our work with teachers and adolescents in an educational social networking project. This three-year design-based research study (Collins, Joseph, & Bielaczyc, 2004) connected young people at sites in Norway, India, South Africa, and the United States, with students and their teachers meeting weekly to create media artifacts to share with others via a private educational social network called Space2Cre8 (S2C8) (for more details, see Hull,

Stornaiuolo, & Sahni, 2010). The social network itself was created and customized over time in response to and coordination with youth and other key stakeholders. The S2C8 network was similar to commercial social networks in that it had a wall, profile pages, chat, private messaging, and other popular communicative features, but it was also multilingual, closed to the general public, and turned toward educational uses. In addition, the research team created a customized data analytics program that provided a variety of detailed log file data, including participation records (e.g., how often participants logged in, from which IP address, how often they viewed a page and for what length of time, their click histories, etc.) and all content generated on the site (e.g., blogs and their revision histories, wall posts, profile images, videos, etc.).

As a design research study, the Space2Cre8 project included a wide range of data collected through an iteratively shaped process responsive to the context of the study. This research paradigm was particularly well suited for the study of networked learning (Stornaiuolo et al., 2013). For example, when the research team learned that youth wanted a way to ask a large number of other students across the networked community about their experiences, the team created a polling feature so that participants could ask the whole S2C8 population questions that intrigued them and then see the answers in multiple representational forms (for an example, see Figure 2). This feature contributed to a shift in the way students communicated, from a one-to-one model of individual question-response toward a more collaborative, connected ethic. The online analytics allowed us to trace who participated and to create response maps that helped us visualize student interactions. This is just one example of how we sought to gather a wide variety of data about participants' interactions in the networked community, which also included detailed online records, participants' multimedia work, formal, informal, and peer-based interviews, and a wide variety of other participant-produced reflective and interpretive artifacts (e.g., digital stories, T-shirt art, community maps).

In addition to serving as the research coordinator for the design based study, Amy conducted a multi-sited ethnography tracing five teachers' practices with educational social networking over two years of the project (Stornaiuolo, 2012). In addition to being one of the researchers at a New York site (for more about this site, see Smith & Hull, 2012), Matt conducted a qualitative study of students' multimodal composing during the intensive summer program. Thus, we were both "located" as participants in the multi-sited project in different ways, complicating and facilitating our work as ethnographers and participants in the networked community. Our own positionality within the research was constantly in our consciousness as we straddled the line between participants and observers. In Amy's study of the teachers in the project, for example, the teachers were part of the research team, members of their school and classroom communities, and participants in her study. The teachers negotiated across these multiple roles in ways that were both deeply enriching and complicated. For instance, two of the teachers kept written teaching reflections that served as useful research records as well as important internal documents guiding their practices (though one stopped part way through the study), one of the teachers was reluctant to write anything, one kept written records private, and another put teaching notes on the web for stakeholders to see. This range of practices raised issues about fair representation and understanding of processes at work – participants take up different roles relative to the research and researchers over time and must be continually negotiated.

Similarly, students were encouraged to take up multiple roles as we asked them to help design the network, to record their own field observations via video, and to imagine new media projects to pursue. While some students took up these invitations to work with us in the field, our overlapping roles as teachers, colleagues, and researchers complicated these efforts and positioned us as the ones with the power to do the inviting. Consequently, some of the participants saw us as helpful collaborators, others kept more of a cautious distance, and still others willingly answered our questions but took no interest in participating in the creation of a research agenda. This constant negotiation of our own positions and identities within the research site is characteristic of multi-sited ethnography in which the researcher's role is itself being mapped "as the landscape changes across sites" (Marcus, 1995, p. 112).

We turn now to consider an example from our project that serves to illuminate the three challenges we identified above – tracing cross-contextual meaning making, managing data multiplicity, and negotiating ethical dimensions of networked research. In the next section we begin with an analysis of a number of conversations about sexuality that emerged in students' digital artifacts, classroom conversations, and online interactions during the summer of 2010, one of the most intense periods of networked participation in the project. We describe our attempts to trace the ways that these discourses around sexuality emerged and circulated across the networked community and how these intersected with students' literacy practices and teachers' pedagogical decisions. In the subsequent section we detail how these emerging and circulating discourses manifested as resonances, which we define as echoes or vibrations across the network, less tangible than intertextual references but identifiable by their reverberations across semiotic systems (cf. Hull et al., 2013). We discuss our efforts to trace these resonances through data collection and analysis, especially our efforts to do so using networked and multimodal tools and practices.

Networked Meaning Making: Exploring Sexuality

The topic of sexuality emerged from our initial thematic analyses of the data from this time period, captured primarily in youth created artifacts, youth chats and messages, and teacher conversations. We also were aware of the lived dimensions of these concerns at the time, as we talked to stakeholders like the project director in India who was concerned that explicit talk about sexuality could put her students, young women who faced tremendous pressure to conform to local gender expectations, at risk. We began to map how the conversations around sexuality emerged in the networked context by locating all of the artifacts

33

referencing the topic. We found that the first publicly posted artifact on the topic was a blog entry by a young woman in New York on "sexual orientation discrimination" (see Figure 1).

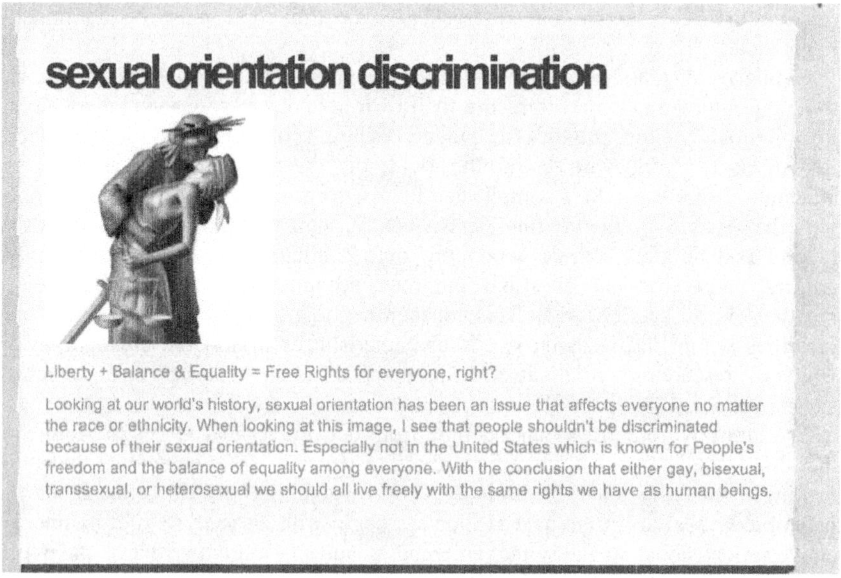

Figure 1. Elena's blog 7/7/10

In her multimodal blog entry, Elena argued that people should not be discriminated against for their sexual orientation and that the United States should be at the forefront of protecting these fundamental human rights. The accompanying photo of the Statue of Liberty kissing the Lady Justice helped to situate her argument about gay rights within a (US) nationalistic framework, but at the same time Elena positioned sexual discrimination as an issue that touched people "no matter race or ethnicity", that is, as a matter relevant to all members of S2C8. The topic remained an important one to Elena throughout the summer program, arising in class discussions about cosmopolitanism (cf. Smith & Hull, 2012) and as the topic of her final digital story. In an interview about her digital story, Elena spoke about how her ideas about sexual discrimination developed through her past experiences with her brother, interactions with her parents on the issue, discussions with classmates, and her participation in the globally-oriented program. In the film, Elena centrally positioned the photo from her blog (Figure 1) amid text slides and snippets of interviews with friends and classmates to explore how sexual discrimination was fundamentally unjust. The opening frame of her film echoed her earlier blog post in situating the issue of sexual discrimination as one that transcended traditional markers of difference, with yellow text on a black background: "Love comes from the heart and when there's love/it does not look for race, age, color NOR gender".

34

Elena worked diligently to make her inquiry into sexual discrimination relevant to her local and global audiences, something that did indeed appear to be taken up by others in the networked community. For example, Shana, one young woman in the New York class, wrote a blog about gay marriage and others referenced Elena's blog post in their discussions of Appiah's (2006) text on cosmopolitanism.

About a week after Elena's blog post, one of Elena's classmates, Victoria, posted a poll about whether "Gay/Lesbian/Bisexual relationships [are] accepted in your society" (Figure 2):

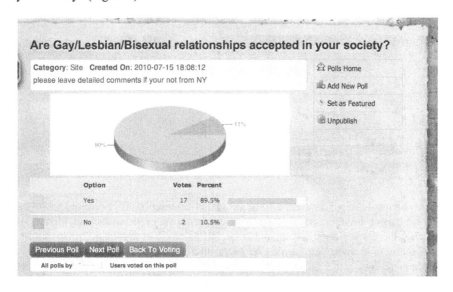

Figure 2. Poll on 15/7/2010

What appeared to be a local issue around sexual discrimination from a US perspective took a global turn in these online conversations and artifacts. Responses and comments on these artifacts revealed that participants from across the different S2C8 sites carefully considered Elena and Victoria's questions in the context of their everyday worlds. For example, responses to the poll from participants in the other New York site, the Oakland site, and the India site included, in part: "Of course they are but they cannot get married"; "In New York where I live these relationships are accepted and they are aloud by law to get married!! I hope the world becomes more open-minded in the near future!"; and "Gay and lesbian relationship are still frowned upon in India". These comments suggested that participants were thinking about issues of sexuality and gender rights in the context of their different cultural belief systems but also in the context of "the world" more broadly.

The ideas around sexual orientation began to blossom across the network shortly after Elena's posting, including a powerful blog in mid-July in which one young

35

woman from our second New York site, Jessica, came out to the networked community as bisexual (see Figure 3).

Figure 3. Opening section of a student blog

Like Elena, Jessica framed the issue of sexual orientation as one relevant to "the world" more broadly, but Jessica drew on her own experiences and identity to anchor the conversation, pronouncing herself as bisexual and using the symbol of the rainbow to signal gay pride. We were interested in the ways that Jessica was influenced by Elena's semiotic efforts and we sought to draw connections between their work in order to illuminate the circulating discourses at play around the theme of sexuality.

As we began to draw connections and intertextual links between students' online texts in relation to our thematic focus, we faced a methodological dilemma. In many cases, we could not find explicit links between young people's texts or online conversations – students' semiotic work in relation to sexuality appeared to emerge in parallel during the same time frame, not clearly linked through the online data. For example, in Elena's New York site, her classmate Shana posted a blog about gay marriage the day after Elena posted her blog, but it appeared from the online analytics that Shana never browsed to Elena's blog page. We wondered about the connection between the two young women who were writing on a similar topic: how did their thinking and writing influence one another? What catalyzed their interest and participation around this topic? We looked at other online data that emerged during this time period across the sites, like the use of "sexy" in usernames in South Africa (e.g., sexyd, sexy_boy) and in compliments to one another or in the description of posted media (e.g., a picture of a pop icon was said to be "sexy") or in the use the term "gay" as a kind of joking slur in private chats with each other in Oakland (e.g., "that's so gay!"). We sought to understand in more detail what was happening around the issue of sexuality, why it appeared salient at that moment in the project, and how the participants were involved in its unfolding. It is to that phenomenon of thematic emergence across networked spaces – what we began to call resonance – that we now turn.

Tracing Resonance

We found that the theme of sexuality was a resonant one for S2C8 community members during this time period, tied to broader discourses about freedom and gender rights that wove across online and offline spaces and permeated participants' conversations. In other words, concerns about sexuality were rooted within widely circulating discourses around youth autonomy and identity that our participants were exploring in relation to other young people from around the world who did not necessarily share the same beliefs and experiences. For example, in India, the young women were quite concerned with early marriage, asking their global interlocutors via poll whether others could choose their partners or marry for love. The young people in South Africa grappled with these questions as well but in a different way. The idea of a dowry, for example, was foreign, but the concept that young women could be forced against their will was familiar; indeed, one young woman wrote a fictional story about a girl who had been raped and her rough road toward achieving a "normal" life as a wife and mother. These discourses about whether young people had the right to control their bodies and hearts permeated the networked community and informed how the participants understood their rights in relation to cultural norms around sexual identities.

By mapping the emergence of the topic of sexuality, we began to see new patterns that linked these broader discourses to the local conversations around Elena's advocacy for gay rights or Jessica's discussion of her bisexuality. In order to "trace" these conversations, we tried to take into account their emergent nature. That is, we were attentive to what Leander and Boldt (2013) call the unbounded, rhizomal relations of literacy practices that are not linear or chronological but emergent in activity. The conundrum, we found, was rendering a process or emergent activity in representational form, preserving the dynamism of movement through time and space without being text-centric. To address these concerns, we drew upon the work of Smith (2013) in layering our data onto a dynamic timeline. Building up layer after layer on this timeline, we began with the log file and network data and added to it data from our ethnographic video, audio, and fieldnotes, our interviews, the students' creative work, the teachers' memos and notes, and our own memos and notes (see Figure 4 for rudimentary example).

What is not clear from this textual representation is that we used multimodal tools to layer the data in relation to one another; the video data from the classroom observation thus articulates with field notes and teacher memos to help us understand how these discourses around identity and autonomy emerged during this period. We wanted to account for how the themes of sexuality emerged over

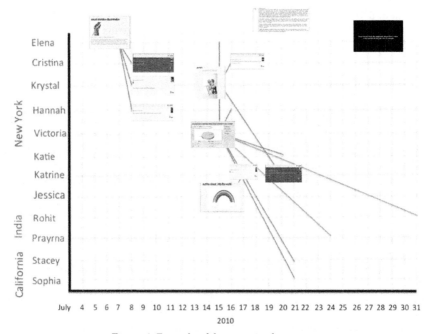

Figure 4. Example of dynamic timeline excerpt

time in ways that were not necessarily connected to one another and that reflected our own positionality. For example, in one of the layers we included how the teachers discussed the issue of sexuality when I (Amy) asked about it during our August meeting, prompted by concerns voiced by teachers in private conversations with me. During that meeting, Amit referenced a conversation with his students about the issue of sexual orientation, which had been precipitated by Jessica's blog about her bisexuality:

> Do you remember that blog entry, Amy? The one about bisexuality? ... We had to come out and make a statement and some of them were unsure what it was. Well, for some of them it's quite a shock, like ... [one girl] was not able to wrap her head around it. (25/8/2010 Teacher Call)

This recounting by Amit was then linked to the field notes and video from the session in which the Indian students discussed bisexuality and Jessica's blog, as well as linked to earlier conversations around sexuality and to young people's online interactions.

This kind of thematic unfolding that we have tried to render methodologically is a central characteristic of what Leander and Boldt (2013) call the constant movement and flux of meaning making, which always involves "a rhythm of continuity and discontinuity, with some possibilities moving toward closure even as others catch fire" (p. 43). We hope to have illustrated how the theme of sexuality "caught fire" in the S2C8 community, not necessarily through direct or implicit referencing across sites, individuals, or artifacts. Rather, we found that the emergence of this theme was tied to historically situated and temporally relevant discourses circulating in the various communities in which S2C8 members participated. These discourses touched an emotional chord, resonating with participants' personal experiences and feelings that amplified the meaning and importance (Immordino-Yang & Damasio, 2007).

Resonance, as echoes and parallels across activity systems, are not easily traced, since they emerge in rhizomatic fashion and do not follow a linear trajectory. To wit, we might examine how videos "go viral", catching fire and spreading because they resonate with people in a particular way, for a specific moment in time, and instantiate broader and more widely circulating cultural, historical, and ideological discourses. Meaning making in networked contexts is characterized by such resonances, which serve to build affinity and highlight connections between people. They can be interactionally built over time between interlocutors (Hull et al., 2013; cf. DuBois, 2007) or emergent from semiotic activity in networked contexts. In the S2C8 community, the topic of sexuality, and by extension youth autonomy and identity, resonated with participants beginning in July 2010, creating a rich semiotic environment that helped to build affinity and foreground connections between participants. Over time, as multiple people took up ideas around sexuality in different forms and ways, the echoes and parallels became amplified, creating tremors in the entire system and leading to youth and teacher action (e.g., the Indian participants led a march against gender violence and made a documentary about their efforts). Resonances from these artifacts and interactions have continued to ripple outward even three years later, as new participants find these archived conversations and returning participants revive conversations. While we studied resonances after they occurred, we believe that identifying and following resonance as it occurs has the potential to enrich analysis of networked interactions and reveal important insights about networked communicative practices. Our task, as we see it, is to reframe our methodological lenses to take into better account how meaning making resonates in networked spaces.

CHALLENGES IN TRACING RESONANCE

It is clear that the complexity of researching meaning making in a world characterized by global, networked flows and constantly emerging technologies requires that we expand our methodologies accordingly. Whether adopting creative (Buckingham, 2009) or visual methods (Pink, 2001), borrowing methods from disciplines like art (Barone & Eisner, 2012), or extending ethnographic methods (Coleman, 2010; Hine, 2000), educational researchers have made a compelling case for how to expand our methodological horizons by becoming what Denzin and Lincoln (2011) call "methodological (and epistemological) bricoleur[s]" (p. 681) who choose from an array of possibilities for developing knowledge of the social world. What we hope to have illustrated here is the need to weave those multiple methodologies together, to create synergy between data collection and analysis and to employ multimodal, networked technologies to do so, in order to address the multidimensional complexities of meaning making now.

One of the most pressing challenges that we attempted to illustrate by tracing resonance across the S2C8 community is the difficulty of tracing movements of people, texts, and ideas across space and time. This cross-contextual meaning making, which often manifests as resonances in networked contexts, remains difficult to address methodologically. Part of the challenge rests in understanding the varied and dynamic perspectives that emerge in networked spaces, especially the resonances that ripple and echo across multiple mobile and interconnected meaning making contexts. When we frame such a dynamic process in two dimensions or render the data collection or analysis static in order to make sense of it, we run the risk of losing the emergent and emotional dimensions of the process. The S2C8 network, with participants making meaning across multiple languages, modalities, and spaces, provided a complex testing ground for exploring this cross-contextual tracing across online and offline spaces using multiple methodologies over time. We suggest that tracing resonance in recursive cycles might be well suited to meaning making's emergent and emotional dimensions, something we could not address because we only came to our realizations after the data was collected.

The second challenge we highlighted was related to the first, and that involves how to address the multiplicity of data available to us. While methodological multiplicity – working across qualitative and quantitative data and using new technologies to collect and represent data – is increasingly supported and encouraged (e.g., Denzin & Lincoln, 2011; Robinson & Mendelson, 2012), it raises difficult questions about how to make sense of the data in relationship to one another. As people make meaning across vast networks of people, spaces, and texts, relying on one method, even an expanded one, does not offer the same explanatory potential as a hybrid cross-section of methods from a diversity of traditions. Since networks are themselves hybrid spaces, characterized by resonance and other complex phenomena, we need methodological approaches that are similarly multidimensional and that help us make sense of complex phenomena like resonance via synthesis across methodologies.

Finally, we must take into account how our participation in these networked spaces implicates us ethically in new ways. One way to address these ethical considerations is for researchers to adopt a reflexive position and to articulate that positionality for the reading public and for our participants. A second way is to make visible our methodological decisions, justifying how and why we navigated the methodological landscape in the way we did (Baym & Markham, 2009; Smagorinsky, 2008).

We hope that by illustrating the difficult challenges we face as researchers investigating practices that are constantly in flux (Gallagher & Freeman, 2011) – using ICTs even as we study others using them – we have extended the notion of an expanded methodological toolkit. No longer merely participant observers, researchers are now technologically complicit, and acknowledging the complexities that this raises offers new possibilities for innovation that require critical dialogue about traditional qualitative practices.

ACKNOWLEDGEMENTS

We would like to express our gratitude to the entire Space2Cre8 research team, but most especially to the leadership of the project director, Glynda Hull. This project was supported by the Spencer Foundation, UC Links, and the Graduate School of Education at the University of California, Berkeley. More information about this project can be found at www.space2cre8.com.

REFERENCES

Appiah, K. A. (2006). *Cosmopolitanism: Ethics in a world of strangers.* New York, NY: W.W. Norton.

Asselin, M., & Moayeri, M. (2010). New tools for new literacies research: An exploration of usability testing software. *International Journal of Research & Method in Education, 33*(1), 41-53.

Bagley, C. (2009). Shifting boundaries in ethnographic methodology. *Ethnography & Education, 4*(3), 251-254.

Barone, T., & Eisner, E. W. (2012). *Arts based research.* Thousand Oaks, CA: Sage.

Baym, N. K., & Markham, A. N. (2009). Introduction: Making smart choices on shifting ground. In A. N. Markham & N. K. Baym (Eds.), *Internet inquiry: Conversations about method* (p. vii). Thousand Oaks, CA: Sage Publications, Inc.

Beneito-Montagut, R. (2011). Ethnography goes online: Towards a user-centred methodology to research interpersonal communication on the internet. *Qualitative Research, 11*(6), 716-735.

Black, R. (2008). *Adolescents and online fan fiction.* New York, NY: Peter Lang.

boyd, d. (2011). Social network sites as networked publics: Affordances, dynamics, and implications. In Z. Papacharissi (Ed.), *Networked Self: Identity, Community, and Culture on Social Network Sites* (pp. 38-57). New York, NY: Routledge.

boyd, d., & Crawford, K. (2011). *Six provocations for big data.* From Oxford Internet Institute's "A Decade in Internet Time: Symposium on the Dynamics of the Internet and Society" (pp. 1-17). Retrieved from http://ssrn.com/abstract=1926431

Buckingham, D. (2009). 'Creative' visual methods in media research: Possibilities, problems and proposals. *Media, Culture & Society, 31*(4), 633-652.

Coleman, E. G. (2010). Ethnographic approaches to digital media. *Annual Review of Anthropology, 39*(1), 487-505.

Collins, A., Joseph, D., & Bielaczyc, K. (2004). Design research: Theoretical and methodological issues. *The Journal of the Learning Sciences, 13*(1), 15-42.

Denzin, N. K., & Lincoln, Y. S. (Eds.). (2011). The future of qualitative research. *The Sage handbook of qualitative research* (3rd edition). Thousand Oaks, CA: Sage Publications, Inc.

Dirksen, V., Huizing, A., & Smit, B. (2010). "Piling on layers of understanding": The use of connective ethnography for the study of (online) work practices. *New Media & Society, 12*(7), 1045-1063.

Du Bois, J.W. (2007). The stance triangle. In R. Englebretson (Ed.), *Stancetaking in discourse: Subjectivity, evaluation, interaction* (pp. 139-182). Philadelphia: John Benjamins.

Gallagher, K., & Freeman, B. (2011). Multi-site ethnography, hypermedia and the productive hazards of digital methods: A struggle for liveness. *Ethnography and Education, 6*(3), 357-373.

Gupta, A., & Ferguson, J. (1997). Discipline and practice: "The field" as site, method, and location in Anthropology. In A. Gupta & J. Ferguson (Eds.), *Anthropological locations: Boundaries and grounds of a field science* (pp. 1-46). Berkeley, CA: University of California Press.

Hine, C. (2000). *Virtual ethnography.* London: Sage.

Hull, G. A., Stornaiuolo, A., & Sahni, U. (2010). Cultural citizenship and cosmopolitan practice: Global youth communicate online. *English Education, 42*(4), 331-367.

Hull, G. A., Stornaiuolo, A., & Sterponi, L. (2013). Imagined readers and hospitable texts: Global youth connect online. In D. Alvermann, N. Unrau, & R. Ruddell (Eds.), *Theoretical models and processes of reading* (6th ed., pp. 1208-1240). Newark, DE: International Reading Association.

Immordino-Yang, M. H., & Damasio A. (2007). We feel, therefore we learn: The relevance of affective and social neuroscience to education. *Mind, Brain, and Education, 1*(1), 3-10.

Ito, M., Gutiérrez, K. D., Livingstone, S., Penuel, B., Rhodes, J., Salen, K., Schor, J., et al. (2013). *Connected learning: An agenda for research and design.* Irvine, CA: Digital Media & Learning Research Hub.

Leander, K. M. (2009). Toward a connective ethnography of online/offline literacy networks. In J. Coiro, M. Knobel, C. Lankshear, & D. J. Leu (Eds.), *Handbook of research on new literacies* (pp. 33-66). New York, NY: Routledge.

Leander, K., & Boldt, G. (2012). Rereading "A Pedagogy of Multiliteracies": Bodies, texts, and emergence. *Journal of Literacy Research, 45*(1), 22-46.

Leander, K., & McKim, K. K. (2003). Tracing the everyday "sitings" of adolescents on the Internet: A strategic adaptation of ethnography across online and offline spaces. *Education, Communication & Information, 3*(2), 211-240.

Lemke, J. L. (2000). Across the scales of time: Artifacts, activities, and meanings in ecosocial systems. *Dynamical Systems, 7*(4), 273-290.

Madden, M., Lenhart, A., Duggan, M., Cortesi, S., & Gasser, U. (2013). *Teens and technology 2013.* Pew Internet and American Life Project. Retrieved from http://pewinternet.org/~/media//Files/Reports/2013/PIP_TeensandTechnology2013.pdf

Marcus, G. E. (1995). Ethnography in/of the world system: The emergence of multi-sited ethnography. *Annual Review of Anthropology, 24*, 95-117.

Pierides, D. (2010). Multi-sited ethnography and the field of educational research. *Critical Studies in Education, 51*(2), 179-195.

Pink, S. (2001). *Doing ethnography: Media, images, and representation in research.* London: Sage.

Robinson, S., & Mendelson, A. L. (2012). A qualitative experiment: Research on mediated meaning construction using a hybrid approach. *Journal of Mixed Methods Research, 6*(4), 332-347.

Smagorinsky, P. (2008). The method section as conceptual epicenter in constructing social science research reports. *Written Communication, 25*(3), 389-411.

Smith, A. (2013, April). *Interactive data visualization techniques for tracing development of writing practices.* Paper presented at the meeting of the American Educational Research Association, San Francisco, U.S.

Smith, A., & Hull, G. A. (2012). Critical literacies and social media: Fostering ethical engagement with global youth. In J. Ávila & J. Z. Pandya (Eds.), *Critical digital literacies as social praxis: Intersections and challenges* (pp. 63-84). New York, NY: Peter Lang.

Soep, E. (2012). The digital afterlife of youth-made media: Implications for media literacy education. *Comunicar, 19*(38), 93-100.

Stornaiuolo, A. (2012). *The educational turn of social networking: Teachers and their students negotiate social media.* Unpublished doctoral dissertation. Berkeley, CA: University of California.

Stornaiuolo, A., & Higgs, J., & Hull, G. (2013). Social media as authorship: Methods for studying literacies and communities online. In P. Albers, T. Holbrook, A.S. Flint (Eds.), *New literacy research methods* (pp. 224-237). New York, NY: Routledge.

Tilley, L., & Woodthorpe, K. (2011). Is it the end for anonymity as we know it? A critical examination of the ethical principle of anonymity in the context of 21st century demands on the qualitative researcher. *Qualitative Research, 11*(2), 197-212.

White, M. L. (2009). Ethnography 2.0: Writing with digital video. *Ethnography and Education, 4*(3), 389-414.

Wiles, R., Crow, G., & Pain, H. (2011). Innovation in qualitative research methods: A narrative review. *Qualitative Research, 11*(5), 587-604.

Amy Stornaiuolo
Graduate School of Education
University of Pennsylvania
USA

Matthew Hall
School of Education
The College of New Jersey
USA

MARTHA BURKLE AND MICHAEL MAGEE

4. RESEARCH CHALLENGES FOR EDUCATION IN VIDEO-GAMES AND VIRTUAL REALITY

INTRODUCTION

For more than a decade now, K-12 and higher education institutions have been exploring the use of video games and other virtual environment technologies to support teaching and learning. Video games have become a ubiquitous part of popular culture. Computers, consoles, and mobile devices have allowed video games to become part of the everyday lives of today's youth (Mitchell & Savill-Smith, 2004). Video games are a significant part of most children's lives today. The arrival of online gaming has resulted in the spread of gaming culture and the creation of a global communication medium. The recent growth of mobile and social gaming has increased the reach of online games into the contexts of daily life.

Unsurprisingly, the persuasive nature of video games has attracted educational researchers interested in the potential of the new medium in teaching and learning (Young et al., 2012). Virtual environments have many similarities with video games. There are several video games such as economic simulators and world builders that provide a kind of "sandbox" where participants can create and explore virtual worlds. Where games tend to include game design elements that focus on achievements, defined challenges and player motivation, virtual environments tend to be created to be completely open. They allow for interaction, exploration and creation, providing a place where users can build exact replicas of famous buildings (for an architecture course), or interact with world-renowned personalities (for a science program), or buy a time share condominium to spend a holiday (for a course in finance). Furthermore, a number of universities around the globe have begun building virtual sets where students could meet to have a coffee, or to exchange academic ideas, or to define a problem for solution, or to consult with their instructor.

The assessment of the potential of new technologies in education has always driven research into news areas. There are other reasons that have encouraged the exploration of new technologies. A new generation of students who have grown up in a digital world are arriving at K-12 and post-secondary institutions. They are adept at utilizing and communicating using technology. Video games and virtual worlds are one attempt to engage this "Net Generation" – and their use of gaming and computer-generated virtual worlds for entertainment – into their programs and

G.B. Gudmundsdottir and K.B. Vasbø (Eds.), Methodological Challenges When Exploring Digital Learning Spaces in Education, 45–61.

course offerings. Examples of these are the beautiful student-centred learning spaces developed in Second Life (SL) by Ohio University, and the Campus Welcome Model built in SL by Athabasca University (Burkle, 2010).

The research into implementing video games and virtual environments in education has not been completely motivated by a need to connect with a new generation. There are also an increasing number of claims about the value of video games and digital environments. Those who see the beneficial results of video games have a long list of positive effects. These include a host of cognitive skills such as an increased ability to problem-solving, to filter misleading perceptual information, to tolerate failure, to exhibit greater creativity in problem solving, and to exhibit higher levels of competitiveness and greater optimism (Bialystok, 2006; Aldrich, 2005).

The impact of these digital environments has been generalized to an entire generation. This gamer generation accepts a chaotic and rapidly changing environment as something normal and expected (Hagood, 2000). The long periods of online video-game play with other gamers has also been observed to lead to an increase in social skills and time management skills (BBC, 2006). Overall, the phenomenon has been termed "the sleeper curve" by Johnson (2005), and he considers it "the single most important new force altering the mental development of young people today" (Johnson, 2005, p. 12). The term came from the observation that the phenomenon was occurring silently in the background and has escaped the notice of society.

Many of these conclusions are based on generalized, intuitive perspectives on what may be occurring during video game play, not formal research. Despite this lack of rigour, many of these observations are beginning to make their way into the popular media as truths, despite never having been examined under any kind of academic scrutiny. There is a growing requirement to examine the claims that video-game play is providing a series of cognitive benefits that are providing gamers with an advantage in the real world. This perspective has resulted in other researchers addressing the same concern about the impact of video games on the rest of a game player's life. The answers aren't simple as recent study found (Stevens, Satwicz, & McCarthy, 2008). The research indicated that the actual impact of video game play is difficult to definitively determine and depends on the individual and the context. Expectedly, there are no simple generalizations that can provide answers for researchers or society about the impact of video game play in the real world. This is a key motivation for examining the wider societal trends of video game play as well as their potential to have a positive impact on education.

In order to move beyond many of the popular anecdotes being presented by the media about video games a more rigorous academic research framework needs to evolve to investigate the claims about video games and virtual reality. This chapter is about the research challenges when building such a framework and how that framework can provide value to the education community in discussing learning and cognitive development. The range of methodological approaches is considerable and this chapter provides two approaches to building research frameworks when examining the challenges for learning in videogames and virtual reality. One approach uses a learner's personal epistemological beliefs (PEB) – understood as an individual's beliefs about what constitutes knowledge and knowing, and learner's identity – understood as how learners present themselves or identified with the created avatar in a virtual environment.

The initial challenge in identifying a research framework to study learning and video games is finding something that has already proven meaningful in describing the growth of an individual's thinking and knowledge-evaluation skills and can still be applied to a video game context. The framework needs to be both meaningful to educational researchers and applicable to the context of video games. The wide variety of video game designs add an additional level of complexity as the context for playing video games can vary considerably. Video game genres, such as adventure, first-person-shooter and role-playing provide a wide range of experience. Delivery platforms such as desktop computer, console and mobile devices provide wide ranging game play contexts.

Personal epistemological beliefs was chosen as an approach to investigating the learning experience in video games as it developed from a researching learning experience in wide range of educational programs within formal educational institutions (Braten & Stromso, 2006). As there has been no previous research into personal epistemological beliefs and video games, the paper reviewed existing literature that comes from educational research (Annetta, Minogue, Holmes, & Cheng, 2009; Clancy, Fazey, & Lawson, 2007).

The wide range of technologies and interactive media has made the definition of games difficult for the game development community. Although heterogeneous, there are some boundaries that can be described to delineate where the research framework could be applied. Wittgenstein's (1958) perspective on the definition of game addressed the idea of defining a concept with vague boundaries. He believed that it was important to be able to discuss concepts that may seem indistinct. This approach is not only applicable but is the only pragmatic way to approach a definition of video games. Rollins and Adams (2003) define a game as a form or interactive entertainment, while Lindley (2003) considers a game as a goal-directed and competitive activity, and Crawford (1982) understands the nature of a game as a self-contained system with explicit rules. Three components appear to be common to most of the definitions: rules, interaction, and space. Most game designers would agree with this very vague definition.

Interesting in researching learning in video games came about when educational researchers began investigating video games and recognized that game designers are thinking about the same sorts of challenges that face teachers and instructional designers involved in teaching and learning (Gee, 2003). The interest has not been necessarily mutual however. Game designers have not reacted positively to the attempt to build a formal academic framework of learning in games (Prensky, 2001). They see the terminology and semantics of the academic community as far too complicated and limiting.

Beyond the definition of a game there is an understanding of the underlying game design. There is a wide range of video game designs available, creating a vast array of game genres to suit players' preferences. A game design is a formal approach that defines game play and how to make it work (Rollins & Adams, 2003). There is no common approach to game development and much of the framework used to implement a game design is implicit and intuitive. Some groups have been working on this in order to improve communication amongst game designers and the team of programmers and artists who need to implement that design. The lack of a mature framework within the game industry points out the relative youth of the discipline but also identifies a limitation in utilizing a comprehensive and detailed language that can be used to discuss it in research.

Games and Education

In reviewing some of the previous research in the use of video games in educational contexts there is a common trend towards researching games that were related to the subject matter curriculum. Not all these video games have been necessarily purpose built for education; there are some commercial off-the-shelf (COTS) that have been used to facilitate learning. Entertainment COTS video games like *Civilization* have been used in educational contexts and can boost interest in historical topics as well as make students aware of the depth of factors related to historical events (Lenhart et al., 2008). There were also games that were specifically built for educational experiences such as *Oregon Trail*, used to teach students about pioneer life, and *Carmen Sandiego*, focused on teaching geography and history. Other studies concluded that using mathematical video games resulted in a more efficient and rapid understanding of the learning outcomes at a wide range of educational levels (Divjak & Tomic, 2011). There are also longitudinal studies that have looked at the video games over a longer period of time. Van Eck (2006) indicated that over 40 years of studies showed that games promoted learning and could decrease the amount time required to teach a subject. Not all of the research on the educational potential of video games has been positive. A recent meta-analysis of the literature indicates that despite the potential of video games to impact education, there is little evidence of it occurring (Young et al., 2012). An important element of that conclusion was that games had limited evidence of solving the problems that occur within the traditional structure of K-12 education.

The mix of both positive and negative perspectives on the educational potential video games is difficult to evaluate. The reason had to do with the limitations of the current methodologies used in educational research not extending to account for many of the unique element offered by video game play (Young et al., 2012). There are several problems that have been identified. Many educators can't find video games that are purpose built for their learning outcomes and educational context. They have looked at the thousands of commercial video games available on the market. They face issues of discoverability of the appropriate game. Even if they find it, they need to be able to evaluate the design that was used to build the game and assessment strategies that are used to gauge the player's success. Most of the frameworks used in education have evolved and matured within the, structured curriculum of formal education. This isn't unique to COTS games, even the games that have been developed with educational purposes in mind are not useful unless the assessment that is built into the game is relevant and meaningful in the educational context in which it is to be used (Mayo, 2009). The lack of credible assessments affects the willingness of many educators to take the time and effort to engage in the use of game-based learning. It also limits the willingness of researchers to spend time researching the learning context of video games.

Personal Epistemological Beliefs (PEB) as a Methodological Framework for Researching Learning in Video Games.

The use of the research domain of personal epistemological beliefs is one approach to finding a relevant research framework for discussing learning and development within video games. The research paradigm of personal epistemological beliefs (PEB) focuses on the growth and development of an individual's understanding of knowledge and knowing. Personal epistemology is an abstract concept that can be discussed without necessarily judging the value of the actual concrete learning experience that underlies an educational experience. In an educational context it separates the process of learning from the knowledge created during learning. It evolved from a qualitative research approach that examined the value of education in a liberal arts college environment. The goal was not to determine what students had learned during their time in college but how their personal epistemology had evolved and matured as a result of the educational experience (Perry, 1999). This separation makes it useful to examine PEB in a video game environment. The process of learning is interesting for educational research, even when the knowledge, such as of the video game, is irrelevant. For example, the encyclopaedic knowledge of an imaginary world would hardly be valuable to a researcher in education. But the process of developing that knowledge is extremely interesting. The next problem is how to use the research paradigm to discuss learning in video games in a meaningful way.

PEB research specifically focuses on how we develop and mature over time and how these affect the way we think about knowledge and knowing. PEB is not interested in the *kinds* of knowledge we develop during a formal education experience but rather how our overall thinking changes and matures during that experience. The belief is that perceptions of learning are reflected in the way students approach a learning situation. As students' PEB grow in sophistication, they become more capable of dealing with complexity and ambiguity. The maturity and sophistication of an individual's PEB have been linked to that individual's effectiveness in learning in complex and ambiguous environments as well as teaching others in inquiry-based educational environments (Spiro, Feltovich, & Coulson, 1996; Clancy et al., 2007). Most of the research describes the growth of PEB as a progression of attitudes towards knowledge. Their perspective toward knowledge begins with a simple, reductivist perspective and evolves to a complex, relativistic perspective.

Examples of how this progression manifests itself include both traditional academic performance and problem-solving ability in ill-structured domains among adult learners (Braten & Stromso, 2006; Spiro et al., 1996). The nature of this progression is the subject of a number of different research perspectives, and there is no immediate consensus on how this progression occurs (Bendixen & Rule, 2004; Hofer & Pintrich, 1997). This progression does not require an individual always to view the world as ambiguous and uncertain, but rather provides freedom for his or her own judgment about when to view knowledge as certain or ambiguous (Chandler, Hallett, & Sokol, 2002; Spiro et al., 1996).

There are a number of research challenges to examining PEB in video gamers. The most obvious one is applying the existing research methodologies of PEB. These methods were created to explore perspectives about knowledge and knowing in a formal, structured educational setting. There have been other research projects that have used the framework successfully to explore personal epistemology in other contexts (Muis, Bendixen, & Haerle, 2006), but the work of Magee (2011) represents the first time it was used to research personal epistemology in a video game context. The highly heterogeneous nature of video game design created an additional complication. There are no formal rules for design and delivery of video games. Unlike most curriculum and educational program designs, the frameworks and underlying philosophies of video game designs are rarely explicit or consistent.

PEB research began as an exclusively qualitative research framework. Quantitative data gathering began as PEB research gained academic acceptance and as researchers began to develop survey instruments. Statistical analysis was utilized to identify and refine patterns in the responses that correlated to the personal epistemological structures identified in the qualitative research (Schommer-Aikins, 2004; Schraw, Bendixen, & Dunkle, 2002).

Data Gathering in Video Games to Support Research Investigation

This brings us to a practical discussion of how to gather data from online video gaming communities that would allow an investigation into their personal epistemological belief structures and thereby their attitudes towards knowledge and knowing. Video games are a communication medium that continues to evolve. They have incorporated a wide range of communication technologies that allow the players to engage in unstructured dialogues with other players. Text-based chats and voice conversations are common in most modern video games. They represent a rich source of data as the players interact with each other by socializing, collaborating on strategy and learning how to be successful in the games. There is also a large amount of data that is created outside of the video game experience. Communities of video gamers will collaborate and discuss their experience in wide range of game community and social media contexts. This means that any research framework can focus on both in-game and post-game contexts to gather data.

When looking to gather data in-game there are some technological challenges. These are: 1) video games are typically proprietary and closed systems; and 2) the nature of much of this data created in the game play is transitory.

Most video game environments are owned by private or public corporations that do not provide access to their games or computer logs. The closed nature of these environments is due to the competitive nature of the industry as well as ethical and privacy concerns around the adults and minors playing the games. Obtaining permission from the company and video gamers to record and analyse their in-game conversations is difficult. The game would first need to be capable of recording all of the text and voice-based conversations and then making them available to the researcher. Voice communications are typically in real-time during the game-play activity; it is streamed between players and never recorded. Chats between players often have a history feature that allows review of past conversations, but those are only available to those in the original conversation.

Even if the researcher were able to obtain all of the data, there would need to be a considerable amount of data-cleaning in order to distinguish which parts of the data were relevant to issues of learning and personal epistemology. A more practical approach would be the use of more directed research methodologies, such as the think aloud approach that has been used when researchers are examining the thought processes of users engaged in technology-mediated environments (Willis, 2008,
p. 71). This approach can be open but can also allow for framing of questions that can guide the thought processes being articulated by the research participant.

There is a considerable amount of non-human readable data created during video game play as well. There are volumes of programming code that capture player behaviour and reactions to that behaviour as part of the game. This represents millions, and likely billions, of data points being collected to reflect the player. The biggest challenge lies in the processing and storage of that player data. The rationale for gathering the data is to provide a positive game-playing experience, not to provide human readable feedback. Most of the data is stored and processed within the program, allowing for the software running the video game to work effectively. Even if the data could be converted to a format that would be useable by a researcher, it would take considerable amount of time to understand what types of data were actually useful for describing the PEB of the gamer. The data structures were never created by the original game programmer with the goal of creating psychometric profiles of the players. It would be difficult not only to determine which data points were relevant, but also which data is only stored for the duration of the game.

A post-game interview provides a chance to discuss the overall strategy that a player has when learning how to play a video game and eventually be a successful player. The use of post-game interviews allows for a multifaceted discussion of the video game environment. The exploratory approach also allows for the discovery and identification of additional elements that influence, and abet PEB when learning to play (Magee, 2011). The weakness of the approach is the reflective nature of the conversations: they often represent a processed and synthesized perspective on how the research participants perceived their learning. It is not a description of their actual experience while it was happening.

Using research instruments to analyse epistemological perspectives towards the video game experience are also possible. The Epistemological Belief Scale (EBS) survey instrument is one example of a research tool that has been used to analyse

PEB structures across multiple educational contexts (Schommer-Aikins, 2004). It was designed to create quantitative data, and began as a tool to analyse undergraduate learning. It has since been modified and validated to work in a range of K-12, adult learning and cross-cultural contexts (Colbeck, 2009). A PEB survey instrument using a similar philosophy could be developed for video games. There is currently no such instrument, and the current EBS uses language that clearly asks about an individual's perspectives towards learning in a formal post-secondary institution. It would be necessary to create a new survey instrument and then run it through rigorous testing to determine whether the underlying components were being consistently identified and measured.

Table 1. PEB research challenges

Research method	*In-game/off-game*	*Data possibilities*	*Research challenges*
Qualitative methods for data gathering	In-Game: Rich dialogue with other players	Text based chats Voice conversations	Video games are typically proprietary and closed systems. The nature of much of this data is transitory. Considerable amount of data cleaning
Qualitative methods for data gathering	Post-Game Interview	Discuss the overall learning strategy with the player: Rich discussion of the video-game environment	The reflective nature of these conversations reflects a processed and analysed perspective, not a description of the player actual experience

ONLINE RESEARCH CHALLENGES IN VIRTUAL 3-D WORLDS:
THE ROLE OF THE AVATAR

Research on PEB is even more challenging in virtual reality (VR), which extends the world of the video game. In video games, and more obviously in VR, the gamers subsume their personalities with a persona or avatar, a computer generated image (digital representations) of oneself used in social virtual environments to interact with others (Schroeder, 1997; Bell, 2008).

The use of the avatar has been examined in the post-secondary environment by Burkle (2010) and Magee (2011). They found that virtual scenarios in the 3-D environment pose many difficulties in gathering data. In the virtual world, when learners interact with each other, with the instructor, and with the learning materials, they do so through their avatars (Garau et al., 2005). Avatars have an agency or capacity to perform actions and interactions, and are controlled, mostly, by a human agent in real time, but provide an element of anonymity.

The capacity that the virtual world offers with regard to anonymity, to mask users' identities, to hide reality, is an issue of concern for researchers in social sciences in general, and in education in particular. Furthermore, gamers in virtual worlds can find themselves in dangerous situations, where they no longer recognize who they are, and where the distinction between themselves as beings and their avatars is no longer clear (Hoorn, Konijn, & Van der Veer, 2003).

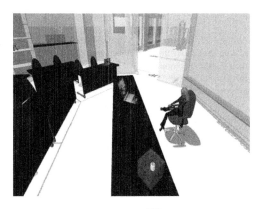

Figure 1. Instructor Avatar in a classroom

And so, students are using these virtual images or digital representations, to attend a class, or to be in a lab practice, or to use a simulation. Behind any avatar there is, therefore, a real person with very basic programming skills, who develop a digital character behind which (or whom) she/he travels the virtual world, builds artifacts, explores spaces, and learns. In a virtual environment developed for the purpose of learning, such as a classroom, or a lab, or a simulation, avatars talk to each other as they touch, discover, see, experiment, and try. Table 2 summarizes the learning possibilities for avatars in learning contexts.

Instructor's Avatar plays an important role in motivating students to engage in the above mentioned learning processes and possibilities. In their work on the effectiveness of Avatar learning, Wang, Chignell and Ishizuka (2007) underline the fact that instructors motivate students to learn as they interact with them in their avatar form appearing as tutors, providing feedback and mentoring opportunities.

Instructor's awareness of the learning possibilities of avatars in virtual worlds has recently emerged as these environments grow in complexity and creativity. Current trends of learning capabilities in virtual reality include the "transfer of pedagogical concepts from other e-environments", the "creation of educational

Table 2. Avatars' learning possibilities

Avatar learning possibilities	Learning context: Virtual classroom	Learning context: Virtual lab	Learning context: Simulation
Attendance	Avatars 'physically' meet in the virtual classroom	Avatars 'physically' attend the virtual lab	Avatars 'physically' meet at the simulated 3-D environment
Course content (theory) learning	Avatars attend a lecture in a virtual environment	Avatars listen to a lab demonstration while they see and interact with objects in the 3-D virtual lab	Avatars can simulate all sorts of procedures and experiences in virtual environments
Interaction with instructor	Avatars ask questions to instructors (either in their Avatar-persona form or in the real presence form)	Avatars learn how to use laboratory equipment by asking questions to their instructor	Avatars learn how to react to a simulation by experimenting the simulated environment
Interaction with learning objects	Avatars use the learning object by using their computer software	Avatars use and design laboratory equipment by using basic programming skills	Avatars learn how to behave in a simulated 3-D virtual environment where the presence of objects is crucial to their learning
Interaction with other learners	Avatars can discuss with each other to sort out a problem in the virtual classroom environment	Avatars learn from their peers as they learn how to use lab equipment, how to solve lab problems, etc.	Avatars interact with one another as they reproduce real situations in a virtual environment
Learning by doing	Avatars learn how to solve physical challenges by building 'real' (3-D virtual) objects	Avatars can interact with objects and learn by doing the experiment by themselves	Avatars learn how to perform a particular professional role by executing the proper behaviour of it.
Critical thinking and problem solving	Avatars learn by themselves or in a team by solving a particular problem in the classroom	Avatars learn by themselves or in a team by solving a particular problem in the lab	Avatars learn by themselves or in a team by simulating how a real person (or character) will solve the problem in real life
Role playing	Avatars develop a particular role in a situation by the acquisition of a character's identity	Avatars learn from each other and from the tools available to play the role	By role playing, avatars learn the way they have to act or take decisions in the context of a particular simulation environment

artifacts for educational purposes", and the "integration with other learning technologies with a view to creating 3D virtual classrooms" (Salmon, 2009).

The first challenge that research into education in a virtual world has to confront is that the subjects in the sample are only graphic representations of the real people about whom PEB are desired. This representation of self by avatars implies that when the researcher is using a survey, or developing a questionnaire, he or she has to face two important challenges: trust and identity verification.

Online Virtual Reality Design Research Challenges

Research design in online virtual environments offers many more possibilities for the researcher who is looking to gather data than does the 2-D video-game environment. In fact, in an educational context, almost all the design done for the virtual environment has the purpose of facilitating learning and engaging the learner in the course content. Authors who have examined the design possibilities maintain the researchers are able to construct environments comparable to real-world learning spaces (Sims Bainbridge, 2009; Davis, Murphy, Owens, Khazanchi, & Zigurs, 2009). For example, virtual learning environments in Second Life or OpenSim can be designed around a learning opportunity or around a community of learners. Such designs may offer the expert the possibilities for formal lab experiments in cognitive sciences or ethnography.

However, because learners and researchers in virtual environments are free to design their own avatars, the main challenge is the identity of participants. One way of controlling avatar design (and therefore the psychological construction of the real user) is for the research designer to build a number of avatars from which the learners can choose. Limiting avatar choices provides a safer and more practical environment from which the collection of data would be easier and more straightforward.

Challenges for Research in Virtual Reality, Not a New Issue

The challenge of trust when doing research in virtual worlds is not new. Shirley Turkle (1995) discussed the construction of online identity: instead of being constrained by the situations of real life, virtual reality users build their own personas in virtual worlds where they become what they want to be. In virtual reality, it is nearly impossible to determine where the genuine characteristics, personality, preferences, ways of seeing the world, etc. are hidden behind the figure that is the subject's ideal. Four years after Turkle's work, another philosopher of science Katherine Hyles (1999) explored the idea of a disembodied being (the avatar) who acts on people's behalf and the serious challenges that this possibility presents for researchers in the social sciences. Hyles argues that, as life becomes "artificial" (posthuman) any possibilities of doing research for social sciences as we understand it, become fake and dubious.

More recently questions of identity and trust in virtual environments have been analyzed by a number of researchers (Ridings, Gefen, & Arinze 2002; Bailenson,

Blascovich, Beall, & Loomis, 2003). In their article about "the mechanics of trust" Riegelsberger, Sasse and McCarty (2005) emphasize the fact that the increasing use of technologies has pushed developers in computer mediated communications (CMC) to design strategies to support identity verification and allow users to ensure transactions are honest and real.

In the context of a virtual world, identity is also linked to another amorphous and flexible concept, the 'sense of place' (Pink, 2011). These are visual locations where avatars can meet. This sensor reality is indeed another challenge for the social ethnographer to a point where a new concept of place needs to be built. In Pink's work, virtual places are understood as abstract terms where things and people are interwoven and related to each other.

Burkle (2011) reports seeing her students' avatars solving a problem in a virtual environment programmed by herself and a colleague, with the purpose of stimulating critical thinking and problem-solving. She noticed that students would spend hours trying to sort out the solution to the problem into the wee hours. She reports having seen the quietest and shiest students suddenly becoming active participants in a discussion forum where their avatars need to discuss a problem or put together a play in a virtual setting. Burkle claims always to be a bit suspicious and careful about collecting data for a research project in the virtual world, or about conducting a survey, or interviewing the students behind their sometimes strange avatars. While Turkle (1995) compared data obtained from her students in virtual worlds with interviews and surveys done fact-to-face, Magee (2011) compared their responses with their grades, or with their real lab performances. Issues of self-identity, and trust, become the most relevant topics of concern when developing research within these synthetic environments, as the creators of Second Life called them (Rymaszewski et al., 2007).

Figure 2. Instructor's Avatar (Photo by Craig Maynard, SAIT)

Table 3 gives some examples of the challenges when applying research methods in virtual environments. These are only examples of what the researchers behind the projects will find in virtual worlds.

Table 3. Research methods and challenges in virtual reality (VR) environments

Research method	Research challenge
Quantitative: Surveys	Are there real users behind avatars responding to the questions? Do the answers a reflection of users' (learners) opinions or points of view? Are the answers a product of single thinking or group thinking?
Quantitative: Questionnaires	Are there real users behind avatars responding to the questionnaires? Do the answers a reflection of users' (learners) opinions or points of view? Are the answers a product of single thinking or group thinking?
Quantitative: Focus Group	Are participants in the 3-D virtual focus group answering the question and interacting with each other in a real way? Are users (learners) conducts and opinions being hidden behind their avatars persona? Is the leader of the Focus Group being respected
Qualitative: Observation	Are the behaviours shown by the learners (avatars) real? Is it possible to observe personal transactions that happen between avatars in real time? Are there any behaviours that avatars are hiding from the researcher?
Qualitative: Ethnography	Can the researcher represented by their avatar develop real fieldwork analysis in the framework of the virtual world? What strategies may the avatar-researcher use to immersed her/himself in the virtual world? How can an avatar-researcher be present 24X7 in a virtual world to collect data from observations, and interactions in the artificial (synthetic) social environment?

EDUCATIONAL RESEARCH IN VIRTUAL ENVIRONMENTS: IS THERE A GENERATION GAP?

With virtual reality technology being embraced mostly by the Net Generation, some may argue that the use of virtual environments presents another important challenge for the educational researcher: the different approaches that instructors (not of this generation) and students have in relation to this new environment.

When we think about North American and European higher education institutions, where a large number of lecturers and professors belong to the so called "baby boomer generation", it is only logical to identify the huge gaps that these two generations have with regard to ease of use, familiarity and fascination with technologies and virtual-worlds use. When the digital learner is comfortable with the use of virtual reality to learn and to interact with the instructor and other learners, the educational researcher might feel in some occasions uncomfortable in building her/his own avatar, in moving around the virtual world or interacting with students' avatars. However, research done in the framework of this chapter, found out that the ease of use of technologies is not always related to age, but to personal interest about the technology and the will to spend time and effort learning how to use it.

CONCLUSIONS

There are both practical and theoretical issues that need to be addressed in undertaking rigorous academic research about the educational uses of digital learning spaces. Although many of the existing research methodologies can still be applied while investigating research issues, technology and digital culture have created many new opportunities and challenges for research. Here are some of them:

– Methodologies are designed for a physical educational institution, not a virtual space
– Identity can be flexible and contextual, making it challenging to transfer educational research findings from the virtual space to a physical one.
– Technology is changing rapidly, altering the way we can interact with research subjects and gather data
– Much of the design behind the technology comes from paradigms outside of education and has very different objectives than, say, instructional or curriculum design. This makes it challenging to identify activities and behaviours that are relevant to educational research. It can also make it difficult to gather data as the original design did not have the goal of gathering evidence of certain behaviours that would be relevant to an educational researcher.

Furthermore, and as technology changes and new research possibilities/challenges are offered to scientists and scholars, we cannot reach definite conclusions as to how digital games and virtual environments are already radically changing the way instructors interact with learners, and how learners acquire knowledge. Comparing virtual environments use for learning to physical ones, the research presented in this chapter found that:

1. Students learning in virtual environments are more engaged to the process of learning, than those learning in a classroom.
2. Students learning in virtual environments do not mind spending a large amount of hours trying to solve a problem, while in the classroom setting, the same student might be waiting for the class time to be concluded.
3. Similar to research findings reported by Caspi, Chajut, Saporta, and Beyth-Marom (2006), this research found that introverted or shy students feel comfortable interacting in virtual environments.

In sum, but we can definitely state the fact that there is a need to build more innovative and strong theoretical structures from which to understand the complex learning dynamics and epistemological frameworks that these virtual scenarios offer.

REFERENCES

Aldrich, C. (2005). *Learning by doing: A comprehensive guide to simulations, computer games, and pedagogy in e-learning and other educational experiences.* San Francisco, CA: Pfeiffer.

Annetta, L.A., Minogue, J., Holmes, S.Y., & Cheng, M. (2009). Investigating the impact of video games on high school students' engagement and learning about genetics. *Computers & Education, 53*, 74-85.

Bailenson, J.N., Blascovich, J., Beall, A.C., & Loomis, J.M., (2003). Interpersonal distance in immersive virtual environments. *Personality and Social Psychology Bulletin, 29*, 1-15.

BBC. (2006). *How gaming is all work and no play.* Retrieved from http://news.bbc.co.uk/2/hi/technology/4774534.stm

Bell, M. (2008). Toward a definition of "virtual worlds". *Journal of Virtual Worlds Research 1*(1). Retrieved from http://journals.tdl.org/jvwr/index.php/jvwr/article/viewFile/283/237.

Bendixen, L. D., & Rule, D. C. (2004). An integrative approach to personal epistemology: A guiding model. *Educational Psychologist, 39*(1), 69-80.

Bialystok, E. (2006). Effect of bilingualism and computer game experience on the Simon task. *Canadian Journal of Experimental Psychology, 60*, 68-79.

Braten, I., & Stromso, H. I. (2006). Epistemological beliefs, interest, and gender as predictors of internet-based learning activities. *Computers in Human Behavior, 22*(6), 1027-1042.

Burkle, M. (2011) Apprenticeship students learning online: Opportunities and Challenges for Polytechnic institutions. *Journal Comunicar, 37*, 45-53. Open University, Catalonia.

Burkle, M. (2010). E-Learning for polytechnic institutions: Bringing e-mobility to hands-on Learning. In M. Ebner, & M. Schiefner (Eds), *Looking Toward the Future of Technology Enhanced Education* (pp. 245- 262). Hershey, PA: IGI Global.

Caspi, A., Chajut, E., Saporta, K., & Beyth-Marom, R. (2006). The influence of personality on social participation in learning environments. *Learning and Individual Differences, 16*(2), 129-144.

Chandler, M. J., Hallett, D., & Sokol, B. W. (2002). Competing claims about competing knowledge claims. In B. Hofer & P. Pintrich (Eds.), *Personal epistemology: The psychology and beliefs about knowledge and knowing* (pp. 145-168). Mahwah, NJ: Lawrence Erlbaum Associates.

Clancy, D., Fazey, J., & Lawson, R. (2007). Personal epistemology and teaching and learning in higher education. *Proceedings of the 30th HERDSA Annual Conference, Adelaide, Australia: HERDSA. Enhancing Higher Education, Theory and Scholarship.* Retrieved from http://www.herdsa.org.au/wp-content/uploads/conference/2007/PDF/R/p236.pdf

Colbeck, D. (2009). *Knowledge genesis: Bridging gaps between learning and understanding.* Unpublished Doctoral Dissertation. School of Computing and Information Systems, University of Tasmania, Tasmania, Australia.

Crawford, C. (1982). *The art of computer game design.* Retrieved from http://www-rohan.sdsu.edu/~stewart/cs583/ACGD_ArtComputerGameDesign_ChrisCrawford_1982.pdf

Davis, A., Murphy, J., Owens, D., Khazanchi, D., & Zigurs, I. (2009). Avatars, people, and virtual worlds: Foundations for research in metaverses. *Journal of the Association for Information Systems, 10*(2), 90-117.

Divjak, B., & Tomić, D. (2011) The impact of game-based learning on the achievement of learning goals and motivation for learning mathematics – Literature review. *Journal of Information and Organizational Sciences, 35*(1), 15-30.

Garau, M., Slater, M., Vinayagamoorhty, V., Brogni, A., Steed, A., & Sasse, M. A. (2003).The impact of avatar realism and eye gaze control on perceived quality of communication in a shared immersive virtual environment. *Proceeding CHI'03 Proceedings of the SIGCHI Conference on Human Factors in Computing Systems.* Retrieved from http://dl.acm.org/citation.cfm?id=642703

Gee, J. P. (2003). *What videogames have to teach us about learning and literacy.* New York, NY: Palgrave McMillan.

Hagood, M. C. (2000). New times, new millennium, new literacies. *Reading Research and Instruction, 39*(4), 311-328.

Hofer, B. K., & Pintrich, P. R. (1997). The development of epistemological theories: Beliefs about knowledge and knowing and their relation to learning. *Review of Educational Research, 67*(1), 88-140.

Hoorn, J. F., Konijn, E. A., & Van der Veer, G. C. (2003). Virtual reality: Do not augment realism, augment relevance. *Human–Computer Interaction: Overcoming Barriers, 4*(1), 18-26.

Hyles, N. K. (1999). *How we became posthuman: Virtual bodies in cybernetics, literature, and informatics.* Chicago, IL: University of Chicago Press.

Johnson, S. (2005). *Everything bad is good for you: How today's popular culture is actually making us smarter.* New York, NY: Riverhead Books.

Lenhart, A., Kahne, J., Middaugh, E., Macgill, A. R., Evans, C., & Vitak, J. (2008). *Teens, video games, and civics: Teens' gaming experiences are diverse and include significant social interaction and civic engagement.* Retrieved from http://files.eric.ed.gov/fulltext/ED525058.pdf

Lindley, C. A. (2003). *Game Taxonomies: A high level framework for game analysis and design.* Retrieved from http://www.gamasutra.com/features/20031003/lindley_01.shtml.

Magee, M. (2011). *Worldview at play: How personal epistemological beliefs interact with video games.* Unpublished Doctoral Dissertation. Graduate Division of Educational Research, University of Calgary, Calgary, Alberta, Canada.

Mayo, M. J. (2009) Video games: A route to large-scale STEM education? *Science, 323*(5910), 79-82.

Mitchell, A., & Savill-Smith, C. (2004). *The use of computer and video games for learning. A review of the literature.* London: UK Learning and Skills Development Agency.

Muis, K. R., Bendixen, L. D., & Haerle, F. C. (2006). Domain-generality and domain-specificity in personal epistemology research: Philosophical and empirical questions in the development of a theoretical framework. *Educational Psychology Review, 18*, 3-54.

Nowak, K. L., & Rauh, C. (2005). The influence of the avatar on online perceptions of anthropomorphism, androgyny, credibility, homophily, and attraction. *Journal of Computer-Mediated Communication, 11*(1), 153-178.

Perry, W. G. (1999). *Forms of intellectual and ethical development in the college years: A scheme.* San Francisco, CA: Jossey-Bass Publishers.

Pink, S. (2011).Visual ethnography and the Internet: Visuality, virtuality, and the spacial turn. In S. Pink (Ed.), *Advances in visual methodology* (pp. 113-130). London: Sage Publications.

Prensky, M. (2001). Digital natives, digital immigrants. *On the Horizon, 9*(5), 1-6.

Riegelsberger, J., Sasse, M. A., & McCarthy, J. D. (2005). The mechanics of trust: A framework for research and design. *International Journal of Human Computer Studies, 62*(3), 381-422.

Ridings, C., Gefen, D., & Arinze, B. (2002). Some antecedents and effects of trust in virtual communities. *Journal of Strategic Information Systems, 11*(3-4), 271- 295.

Rollings, A., & Adams, E. (2003). *Andrew Rollings and Ernest Adams on game design.* Indianapolis, IN: New Riders.

Rymaszewski, M., Au, W. J., Wallace, M., Winters, C., Ondrejka, C., & Batstone-Cunningham, B. (2007). *Second life: The official guide.* Indianapolis, IN: Wiley Publishing Inc.

Salmon, G. (2009). The future for (second) life and learning. *British Journal of Educational Technology, 40*(3), 526-538.

Schommer-Aikins, M. (2004). Explaining the epistemological belief systems: Introducing the embedded systemic model and coordinated research approach. *Educational Psychologist, 39*(1), 19-29.

Schraw, G., Bendixen, L., & Dunkle, M. (2002). Development and validation of the epistemic belief inventory (EBI). In B. Hofer & P. Pintrich (Eds.), *Personal epistemology: The psychology of beliefs about knowledge and knowing* (pp. 261-275). Mahwah, NJ: Lawrence Erlbaum Associates.

Schroeder, R. (1997). Networked worlds: Social aspects of multi-user virtual reality technology. *Sociological Research Online, 2*(4).

Spiro, R. J., Feltovich, P. J., & Coulson, R. (1996). Two epistemic world-views: Prefigurative schemas and learning in complex domains. *Applied Cognitive Psychology, 10* (7), 51-61.

Sims Bainbridge, W. (2009). The scientific research potential of virtual worlds. *Science, 317*(5837), 472-476.

Reed, S., Satwicz, T., & McCarthy, L. (2008). n-Game, In-Room, In-World: Reconnecting video game play to the rest of kids' lives. In K. Salen (Ed.), *The ecology of games: Connecting youth, games, and learning* (pp. 41-66). Cambridge, MA: The MIT Press.

Turkle, S. (1995). *Life on the screen.* New York, NY: Simon and Schuster.

Van Eck, R. (2006) Digital game-based learning: it's not just the digital natives who are restless, *EDUCAUSE Review, 41*(2), 16-30

Wang, H., Chignell, M., & Ishizuka, M. (2007, October). *Improving the usability and effectiveness of online learning: How can avatars help?* Paper presented at the Human Factors and Ergonomics Society 51st Annual Meeting, Baltimore, Maryland, U.S.A.

Willis, J. (2008) *Qualitative research methods in education and educational technology.* Charlotte, NC: Information Age Publishing.

Wittgenstein, L. (1958). *Philosophical investigations.* Oxford: Basil Blackwell Ltd.

Young, M.F., Slota, S., Cutter, A.B., Jalette, G., Mullin, G., Lai, B., Simeoni, Z., Tran, M., & Yukhymenko, M. (2012). Our princess is in another castle: A review of trends in serious gaming for education. *Review of Educational Research, 82*(1), 61-89.

Martha Burkle
Centre for Distance Education
Athabasca University
Canada

Michael Magee
Faculty of Education
University of Calgary
Canada

PART II

CHALLENGES FOR RESEARCHER INTERACTION IN VARIOUS LEARNING SITES

GREGORY T. DONOVAN

5. OPENING PROPRIETARY ECOLOGIES

Participatory Action Design Research with Young People

INTRODUCTION

In this chapter I outline a multidimensional approach to doing participatory action design research (PADR) with young people learning in what I theorize as "proprietary ecologies". Proprietary ecologies are the multidimensional ecosystems of privatized data flows within which everyday life increasingly takes place. I use proprietary strategically to describe media that is privately owned and controlled through capitalist property regimes such as trademarks, copyrights, and patents. I theorize this as an "ecology" because the concept bridges an IT discourse of information systems that interact at various scales (i.e. information ecology) with a spatial understanding of the relations of production and reproduction at various scales (i.e. political ecology). In the contemporary knowledge economy, corporations and governments rely on capitalist property models to enclose and control access to the production of knowledge. I doing so, ecologies of platforms and practices are constructed to build knowledge through everyday interactions with media, such as social networks, without giving those generating the data much stake in the process.

The productive and entertaining promises of proprietary communication, education, and play media in postindustrial societies have led to widespread adoption among youth whose daily activities now generate troves of data that are mined for profit. As young people learn to text, email, browse, and search within such environments, their identity configurations link up with informational modes of capitalist production. This places them at the fore of complex cultural negotiations over privacy, property, and security (cf. Donovan, 2014). The enclosure and monetization of young people's personal data is presupposed by and intertwined with privatization happening elsewhere in the structuring of cities, schools, and homes. I begin this chapter with a critical consideration of the methods designed to produce knowledge from, and on, youth for private interests. I then discuss how participatory research and design with youth presents methodological challenges that, when met, help build capacities for critiquing and engaging private modes of knowledge production. In both cases, I draw from interviews and workshops conducted as part of The MyDigitalFootprint.ORG Project (hereafter, The MyDF Project).

G.B. Gudmundsdottir and K.B. Vasbø (Eds.), Methodological Challenges When Exploring Digital Learning Spaces in Education, 65–77.

The MyDF Project entailed 15 interviews with young people in New York City and a collaboration with five youth co-researchers, ages 15 to 19. I worked with these co-researchers, who called themselves the Youth Design and Research Collective (YDRC), to develop an open source social network during eight workshops over a span of six months. The aim of the interviews and subsequent workshops were to understand and engage the ways privatization operates in young people's media environments. I use this PADR project to unpack the platforms and practices that helped the YDRC and me investigate, and ultimately translate, their media experiences into actionable knowledge. By engaging young people as research participants and media producers they developed more critical and multidimensional understandings of privacy, property, and security. Through their involvement in both knowledge and media production, participants came to see ICTs as one dimension of a broader built environment that could be (re)built to afford more open and representative information ecologies. The following sections provide a framework for considering youth development within proprietary ecologies, an outline of the MyDF Project's methodological approach, and a discussion of the research relationships that helped demystify and rework the YDRCs relations with media.

THEORETICAL FRAMEWORK

The expansion of ICTs in the early 21st century has afforded an information ecology that infuses routine behaviors with market interests and unsettles industrial conceptions of privacy, property, and security. Castells (2000, 2003) theorizes the material infrastructure of such ICTs as an informational mode of capitalist development characterized by recombinant abilities, expanding processing capacities, and flexible distribution. Castells (2003) discusses this "informationalism" as a technological paradigm that restructures industrial capitalism and provides the material conditions for a new social structure he calls "the network society" (p. 10). While I hold on to Castells' formulation of informationalism as a restructuring technological paradigm, I wish to critically consider how it plays out in young people's learning spaces as a social and material process rooted in a neoliberal history of accumulation by dispossession. Harvey (2010) sees privatization as a primary mode of accumulation in the contemporary neoliberal state, serving to enclose the public commons and consolidate class power. Harvey notes that this process is different but not detached from accumulation through the exploitation of labor, as accumulation by dispossession produces capital through the enclosure of public resources and subsequent regulation of access to such resources.

In a digital context, Andrejevic (2007) analyses the ways information becomes enclosed and thus commodified to create common resources that people must increasingly pay to access. Similarly, Hunter (2003) argues that we're experiencing a "Cyberspace Enclosure Movement" whereby "private interests are reducing the public ownership of, and public access to, ideas and information in the online world" (p. 3). The consequences of what Andrejevic theorizes as "digital enclosure", and Hunter as a "Cyberspace Enclosure Movement" were often referenced in my interviews and was acutely articulated by 15 year old Megan when asked what concerned her most about the internet:

> That one day, like, nothing will be possible without internet because I feel like that's the age that's coming really soon. They say it's going green, but what is the cost of going green? What about the people who can't afford the internet or computers and how are they going to function? That means that's extra money coming out of their pockets to use someone else's Internet and computer services and things like that.

Who and what is left out of the geography of informational development, or forced to sacrifice more to access and navigate it, concerns Megan. The material social relations that are fostered, or not, by "going green" suggests to her that there are socioeconomic consequences to such dispossession. Many of the young people I interviewed navigated broken home computers, heavily filtered school computers, lost, stolen, or broken mobile phones, as well as expensive monthly bills so they could maintain access to the internet. At the same time they depended on "no-fee" services like Gmail and Facebook to communicate while their schools committed a growing portion of shrinking budgets to proprietary software and services from corporations like News Corp, Blackboard and Apple. This made them attuned to the precariousness of connectivity, the consequences of being unable to access certain information, and the increasing reliance on information companies to live and to learn.

Proprietary ecologies help consolidate class power by privatizing flows of information within a fragmented geography unevenly connected by ICTs. Whether young people facilitate their own social networks, or outsource their networking to corporations such as Facebook, significantly shapes their participation and control over the knowledge produced from their networking. Such ecologies are thus the medium and the method of accumulation by dispossession in an informational context. Although empowerment is possible it remains a material social process and thus calls for a dissolving of dualisms and a building of multidimensional understandings to realize its potential. This means considering how proprietary media such as Google or Facebook can afford empowerment, domination, or both and neither depending on the situated practices that create and make use of them.

SITUATING YOUTH

According to the Pew Internet & American Life Project, 77% of US youth ages 12 to 17 have a cell phone (Lenhart, 2012), while 95% have internet access and 80% of those with internet access use social media sites (Lenhart et al., 2011). According to a Nielsen Ratings report measuring all US mobile phone users, data consumption is strongest among young people ages 13 to 17 with a monthly average of 320MB in 2011, a 256% increase over 2010 monthly averages (Nielsen Wire, 2011). Texting was the most popular data consumption activity, with 13 to 17 year olds exchanging an average of 3,417 messages per month. This intense level of texting was referenced in several of the interviews I conducted. At 16, Nicole found it easier to articulate when and where she doesn't text then when and where she does:

I don't text while I'm sleeping, so that's – that would be the only time unless my phone dies, or I'm in a meeting like this, or I'm playing soccer for a while. The times like that where I, I physically can't text, like those would be the only times where I'm just not texting.

Texting for Nicole is a routinized practice; the absence of which is more notable than its presence. The reciprocity of this data generation and consumption loop tightly couples psychosocial development with a transnational informational development.

This hybrid development means young people increasingly embody Haraway's (1985) metaphorical cyborg through their psychosocial configuration with and within information systems. As Schuurman (2004) argues, cyborgs have become "more than metal and flesh; they come to life in the presence of data" (p. 1337), and their "peer status is established by common data-collection practices, shared goals, and a similar vocabulary" (p. 1339). Young people's modes of knowing and becoming in proprietary ecologies are thus infused with privatized practices such as texting, following, friending, liking, and emailing that shapes this generation's understandings and expectations of privacy, property, and security.

According to Katz (2004), social reproduction "encompasses that broad range of practices and social relations that maintain and reproduce particular relations of production along with the material social grounds in which they take place" (p. X). Such an understanding of social reproduction provides an ecological framework for considering the structural continuity and discontinuity of privatization by accounting for the reciprocal relationships of production and reproduction sustaining it. While social reproduction has often been separated from production, as phenomena distinct from and secondary to the economic realm and the paid labor it constitutes, such conceptual distinctions obfuscate the productive yet unpaid labor often carried out by women and youth, among other others (cf. Mitchell, Marston, & Katz, 2003). Although such a clearly defined distinction was never functional, its dysfunction is emphasized in the context of proprietary ecologies where the continuous circulation of data generated through playful and routine practices is increasingly commodified. In a context where social networks are corporations, and personal information is a commodity; production and social reproduction are overtly and dialectically bound.

In the context of US youth, proprietary ecologies operate in their material social experiences at all scales from the intimate to the global long before they enter the workforce as paid labor. The widespread adoption of proprietary media ties youth ever closer to an informational mode of development as they learn, work, and play, among many other common mediated activities (Donovan & Katz 2009). These ecologies are presupposed by and intertwined with privatization happening elsewhere in the US; from the enclosure and gentrification of urban spaces (Low, 2006; Katz, 1998; Smith, 1996), to the neo-liberalization of education systems

(Fine & Ruglis, 2009; Monahan, 2006), to the governance and financialization of housing (Saegert, Fields, & Libman, 2009; Low, Donovan, & Gieseking, 2012).

Corporations such as Facebook and Google facilitate young people's interactions while simultaneously privatizing them through a dialectical process of informational accumulation and dispossession. While a number of scholars have theorized an ecological approach to the study of media (cf. Postman, 2000; Capurro 1990), I specifically theorize proprietary ecologies as a way of focusing this approach on the myriad and historical ways privatization plays out in the situated interactions of people, places, and media to regulate access to knowledge. As such, The MyDF Project sought to involve youth in designing information systems within their environment so as to involve them in everyday practices of research and knowledge production.

METHODOLOGICAL APPROACH

The MyDF Project's methodological approach aimed to involve young people in collaborative processes of research and reflection through the co-design of an open source social network. My aim as the project facilitator was to understand how routine engagements with proprietary media shape the situated knowledges produced and reproduced around young people's privacy, property and security. I was also interested in what sort of interactions young people wanted to amplify and reduce through their own media research and design. Integral to this process was identifying and addressing what skills and literacies the YDRC needed to design a social network. These were the broad questions explored in interviews with young people, unpacked in workshops with youth co-researchers, and ultimately acted upon through the co-design of a social network (an interactive timeline of the project can be found at http://mydigitalfootprint.org/timeline).

The MyDF Project combined both participatory action research (PAR) and participatory design (PD). A PAR approach opens up the research process to everyday people in order to collectively produce knowledge that addresses problematic situations in their own lives (cf. Appadurai, 2006; Fine et al., 2003). A PD approach opens up the design process to everyday people so as to produce more responsive and democratic objects and built environments (cf. Bannon & Ehn 2013; Greenbaum & Loi, 2012). Both PAR and PD consider knowledge to be rooted in social relations and most actionable when collaboratively produced. The participatory thrust of both approaches present a critical praxis for opening proprietary ecologies. How Facebook chooses to design their user interface is akin to how a social scientist chooses to design a survey protocol. Combining PAR and PD praxis helps to rework the hierarchical power structure of most research and design by challenging who gets to produce knowledge, how, and towards what ends.

Through its research and design politics, a participatory action design research (PADR) approach offers a counterweight to the platforms and practices of proprietary ecologies. Instead of producing new knowledges through privatized means that are largely mystified to all but their owners, a participatory approach counters this knowledge production by opening up regimes of ownership and involving 'users' in the means of production. With information systems now a core component of urban development, PADR has been drawn on to research and design urban infrastructures according to community interests and concerns (cf. Bilandzic & Venable, 2011; Foth & Adkins, 2006). In the context of urban youth, this means unpacking the knowledge produced through their engagements with and within proprietary ecologies and then collaboratively designing a medium and a methodology that reworks this production for their own interests and concerns.

Fine et al. (2003) note the ways PAR has lost its politics overtime to become more a series of techniques. Cognizant of this history, The MyDF Project focused on understanding and addressing young people's media concerns, challenging their modes of knowledge production, and critically appropriating existing PAR and PD methods, or developing new ones, that could help achieve these goals. To involve young people in shaping the project, New York City youth were first involved as research participants through interviews and then as co-researchers in a series of workshops.

1-on-1 Interviews

Interviews with 15 young people provided an opportunity to explore individual experiences, interpretations, and concerns regarding key issues and questions. Information on the MyDF Project, how to participate as an interviewee and/or co-researcher, and an overview of participants' rights were organized into a participant recruitment website. This link was then circulated by contacts that worked with NYC youth in various educational and professional settings. In the month that the recruitment site was active it generated 53 requests to participate. Of those, 22 interviews were scheduled based on the participant's age, location, and availability. Fifteen of the 22 interviews scheduled were conducted. The discrepancy between those interviews scheduled and conducted were due to no shows. Of the interviewees, five were men and 10 were women. One participant was 14, three were 15, four were 16, one was 17, one was 18, and five were 19. Nine lived in Brooklyn, three in Manhattan, two in the Bronx, and one in Queens.

The semi-structured format of the interview explored how participants interacted with ICTs on a daily basis, what role ICTs had in their work and play, and what issues they constructed or didn't construct as matters of privacy, property, and security. This allowed a more free flowing exchange where participants were able to talk about something they knew well, their routines, and reflect on why they did them, how they felt about them, and what if anything was concerning about them. As Crouch and McKenzie (2006) argue, such a small sample qualitative approach "is therefore clinical, involving as it does careful history-taking, cross-case comparisons, intuitive judgments and reference to extant theoretical knowledge" and "positively calls for a collection of respondents' 'states', the size of which can be kept in the researcher's mind as a totality under investigation at all stages of the research" (p. 493). As such, these interviews offered a way to explore and compare individual understandings with one another and analyze them in the context of more generalized and popularized understandings of privacy, property and security.

Research and Planning Workshops

Of the 15 young people interviewed, 11 expressed interest in participating as youth co-researchers and producing an open source social network that further investigated the common concerns and interests voiced in the interviews. Thanks to a small research grant I could afford to compensate eight co-researchers for a limited number of workshops, and thus only eight of those 11 were offered positions. In selecting these eight, I considered their age and level of interest, as well as the interests and concerns they discussed in their interview and how these factors would contribute to a dynamic and diverse grouping. These eight participants were asked to participate in a two-hour project orientation before committing to the position. The reason for an orientation was to give participants a better sense of how the project would operate, to consider their role in it more fully, and to imagine how the project might progress before asking them to commit to anything. Six of the invited participants attended the orientation with five choosing to continue on as co-researchers and one declining citing a demanding extracurricular schedule. Together, the YDRC and I scheduled six research and planning workshops for collaborative research and design.

ENGAGING RESEARCH RELATIONSHIPS

Our research and planning workshops took place at the CUNY Graduate Center in midtown Manhattan. These workshops provided an opportunity to engage the YDRC in investigating and responding to their own interests and concerns as well as those that emerged from interviews. To critically investigate the proprietary ecology of daily interactions we also had to consider interactions within our own research. Luttrell (2010) emphasizes this reflexivity as a centerpiece of the qualitative research and design process that "makes visible the central role that research relationships play", arguing that "negotiating and representing research relationships – what and how we learn with and about others and ourselves – is the heart of the research journey" (p. 160). In proprietary ecologies, daily interactions are research relationships, albeit not ones that are generally visible to the users who double as research subjects. By reflexively analyzing and negotiating the research relationships within our project we were actively producing new connections that countered, paralleled, and reworked those produced through proprietary research. Making visible our own research relationships also helped to identify the skills and literacies we needed to conduct our research and design plans.

Along with tutorials on media and research literacies, the workshops also provided an orientation to the front-end and back-end of the WordPress and BuddyPress software installed on a server to run our social network. WordPress is a free and open source content publishing platform that is capable of generating an unlimited number of networked blogs much how proprietary blogging services such as Blogger or WordPress.com operate. BuddyPress is a free and open source platform that adds common social networking features to WordPress, such as social profiles, status updates, activity feeds, and groups.

Throughout these workshops we drew on Cahill's (2007) "collective praxis" approach to establish "a set of rituals that facilitated deep participant involvement and collective ownership over the research process" (p. 304). This practice was important because ownership over the research process is ownership over the means of knowledge production, a primary matter of concern in proprietary ecologies. While Cahill (2007) practiced writing as one such ritual in her work with young women of color growing up amidst gentrification on Manhattan's Lower East Side, the YDRC primarily practiced media production as a ritual that facilitated collective ownership of our research medium (i.e. our social network). Designing the social network oriented the YDRCs experiential continuum (Dewey, 1938) through a set of practices and rituals so that new experiences would draw from what was learned during previous experiences.

In designing profiles for our social network we had to research how our own social profiles on networks such as Facebook were designed. This allowed us to critically reflect on what questions profiles ask and how people answer them. Ultimately we decided what questions we wanted to ask and why, and then collaboratively designed profile fields accordingly. When Facebook only allows users to indicate their "sex" as "male" or "female" from a drop down menu, they do so to box people into predefined marketing demographics. Users are left with three options: designate your sex as male, female, or leave the field empty. As the YDRC was more interested in knowing how our participants choose to identify their gender, if at all, we decided to make an optional profile field called "gender" that allowed participants to fill in whatever answer they felt most appropriate and then indicate whether this profile field should be visible to other participants or kept private so that only myself and the YDRC could see it. This practice helped us see how social profiles generated "data" on the back-end of our medium, thus prompting new discussions about, and research into, what Facebook might see on their back-end. We developed shared vocabularies and experiences through the research and design process that facilitated our collaborative work while giving the YDRC greater ownership of our medium. In this way, we followed a participatory design that was both cooperative and pragmatic in its approach to understanding our interactions with media (McCarthy & Wright, 2004).

The transition from interviewing young people to conducting research and design with youth co-researchers signaled not only a methodological shift in the project but also a bureaucratic restructuring of the project. Having initially received approval from my university's IRB to involve youth as "research participants" in the project, it was necessary to file an amendment to my application that added each member of the YDRC as "research personnel" so they could officially conduct and analyze academic research with me.

This amendment process required that the YDRC be certified in human subjects research through the successful completion of seven online modules on research and ethics offered by the Collaborative Institutional Training Initiative (CITI)

Program. I led 30-minute tutorials before each of the first three research and planning workshops. During these tutorials we would collectively read and discuss two modules before taking the online multiple-choice tests that followed each section. Two YDRC members who had previously been co-researchers on a PAR project had already received this certification. This was critical as they were able to assist me in facilitating the tutorials while also making clear to the other YDRC members that, yes, this was doable.

This amendment process afforded reflexive analysis. As researchers and producers, the YDRC reflected on how to redesign the relations that typically involved them as subjects and consumers. If this is the kind of oversight our academic research was to be subjected to, what sort of oversight is Facebook's research subjected to? In short, having to consider and reflect on the ethics of our own research relationships provided opportunities and vocabularies for discussing research ethics in proprietary ecologies and thus shaped new multidimensional understandings of privacy, property and security.

Cogitation Workshop

A cogitation workshop was conducted two months after our last research and planning workshop to give the YDRC a chance to reflect on and evaluate our participatory research, group discussions and analysis, and collaborative design process. Together, we discussed what parts of the social network should be made public, and what methods we should use for contextualizing and anonymizing this public content. The cogitation followed a focus group structure where areas of agreement as well as disagreement on issues and statements were explored to analyze the frameworks of thinking underlying those opinions and experiences (cf. Glick, 1999).

Figure 1 was projected during the cogitation workshop to assist the YDRC in reflecting on the dimensionality of everyday experience. As facilitator, I generated this visual following a group reading of Berners-Lee's (1999) description of the web as having four layers and our subsequent discussion of how these layers are experienced on a daily basis. On the left are four layers of the web on the right are four dimensions of the self. The middle column considers one corporation, Apple, and how their content, software, hardware, and transmission products interact with their consumers' experiences at various dimensions. Although the web and the self does not break down so neatly into four dimensions with four corresponding layers, this approach helped the YDRC consider that there were indeed layers and dimensions to their mediated experiences. As corporations develop elaborate vertical integration strategies that angle for greater access to and influence over consumers, recognizing these seemingly disconnected products as integrated aspects of a single business model becomes crucial to demystifying production and unpacking mediation.

Through their involvement in The MyDF Project, the YDRC developed critical capacities for participating in acts of knowledge production through research and design. By engaging their own information ecologies, the YDRC considered aspects of their psychosocial development in relation to broader socioeconomic development. Designing an open source network that was approved by our university's Institutional Review Board (IRB) and that operated at each of Berners-Lee's (1999) four layers of the web provided a series of openings for multidimensional considerations of how information systems do and could operate in one's environment. Berners-Lee's notion of "content" evoked an intimate dimension, "software" evoked a cultural dimension, "hardware" evoked a local dimension, and "transmission" evoked a translocal dimension. Each dimension was a starting point for broader consideration. While software was considered to primarily evoke a cultural dimension, this was but one aspect of software alongside intimate, local, and translocal dimensions.

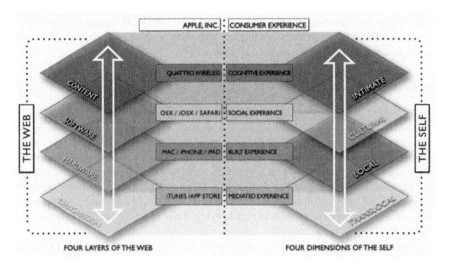

Figure 1. The web and the self

The act of social media production, by which I mean installing, configuring, designing, and managing a WordPress and BuddyPress installation on a private server, afforded a multidimensional consideration of how social networks such as Facebook operate by bringing co-researchers into contact with more than just the user's interface. In learning how to design a social network, the YDRC learned skills and developed insights for reorienting information ecologies towards their own situated interests and concerns.

CONCLUSION

A PADR approach helps expose and express the relations and perspectives most neglected by the media and methods that produce proprietary ecologies. The transition from consumer to producer and researched to researcher prompted constructive breakdowns. These breakdowns unsettled the co-researchers' previous understandings of privacy, property, and security by excavating what they did not know and allowing it to be brought under the gaze of critical inquiry. Having to figure out how to develop a Terms of Use policy, how to design a social profile interface, and how to securely store and annonymize participants' personally identifiable information (PII) led to technosocial breakthroughs. Technically, the YDRC gained new media skills and literacies. Socially, they began to critique Facebook's long and complicated Terms of Use Policy and question what kinds of PII corporations and governments were aggregating, why, and how they were storing it.

The YDRC built a social network using open source software but also proprietary hardware, private domain names, and leased server space. While our specific focus on open source helped the YDRC develop understandings of how proprietary software operated by comparison, our main focus was on opening up our own research relationships (cf. Luttrell, 2010) and configuring an information ecology that could account for the YDRCs multidimensional and often contradictory expectations of privacy, property, and security. An open source publishing platform such as WordPress was technically essential and epistemologically important to this process, but it was the participatory process itself that allowed us to build a more open ecology. As these are ecologies, the distinction between 'open' and 'proprietary' rests in the quality of interactions afforded by each. Whereas proprietary ecologies strive for ownership and often the ownership of user data, an open ecology orients itself towards affinity to collectively organize data flows around the shared interests and concerns of those participating. It is thus more than the source that should be kept open, particularly for youth who are just beginning to negotiate complex identity configurations. It is the means of production entailed in, and revolving around, these informational sources that are being enclosed through modes of dispossession. Information, data, and knowledge once considered outside the domain of property are now being brought into the fold of capitalist production and at a time when their empowering potential is heightened by diminishing costs of interpersonal communication and data processing.

There was excitement among co-researchers that there was an open source software that could be drawn on to build a familiar social network but for different purposes. That the YDRC had to learn about Secure Socket Layer (SSL) certificates and a two-step registration process to comply with IRB requirements for enhancing participant privacy, made them aware and encouraged that their privacy could also be enhanced by similar means. In building a social network, the YDRC built capacities for opening and engaging their own information environment while realizing commonalities between what they expected in terms of privacy, property, and security and what situated others expected. This lead them to design a social network more in line with their own values, but it also turned their attention to dimensions of their environment previously unconsidered. Considering The MyDF Project, I argue that when young people are engaged in research and design their consciousness within proprietary ecologies expands. Such consciousness encourages young people to see themselves as self-possessed social actors, while also affording a multidimensional framework for youth to collaborate meaningfully with researchers, policymakers, designers, educators, and other actors to develop more open ecologies that are sensitive to their interests and concerns.

REFERENCES

Andrejevic, M. (2007). Surveillance in the digital enclosure. *The Communication Review, 10*, 295-317.

Appadurai, A. (2006). The right to research. *Globalisation, Societies and Education, 4*(2), 167-177.

Bannon, L. J., & Ehn, P. (2012). Design: Design matters in participatory design. In J. Simonsen & T. Robertson (Eds.), *The Routledge international handbook of participatory design* (pp. 37-65). New York, NY: Routledge.

Berners-Lee, T. (1999). *Weaving the web: The original design and ultimate destiny of the World Wide Web by its inventor*. San Francisco, CA: Harper Business.

Bilandzic, M., & Venable, J. (2011). Towards participatory action design research: Adapting action research and design science research methods for urban informatics. *The Journal of Community Informatics, 7*(3). Retrieved from http://eprints.qut.edu.au/48110/.

Cahill, C. (2007). Doing research with young people: Participatory research and the rituals of collective work. *Children's Geographies, 5*(3), 297-312.

Capurro, R. (1990). Towards an information ecology. In I. Wormell (Ed.), *Information and Quality* (pp. 122-139). London: Taylor Graham.

Castells, M. (2000). *The rise of the network society* (The information age: Economy, society and culture, Volume 1). Oxford: Blackwell Publishers Ltd.

Castells, M. (2003). The interaction between information and communication technologies and the network society: A process of historical change. *Coneixement I Societat, 1*, 8-21.

Crouch, M., & McKenzie, H. (2006). The logic of small samples in interview-based qualitative research. *Social Science Information, 45*(4), 483-499.

Dewey, J. (1938). *Experience and education*. New York, NY: Touchstone.

Donovan, G. T. (2014). iLearn: Engaging (in)formal learning in young people's mediated environments (pp. 270-281). In S. Mills & P. Kraftl (Eds.), *Informal education, childhood, and youth: Histories, geographies, practices*. Basingstoke: Palgrave Macmillan.

Donovan, G. T., & Katz, C. (2009). Cookie monsters: Seeing young people's hacking as creative practice. *Children, Youth and Environments, 19*(1), 197-222.

Fine, M., & Ruglis, J. (2009). Circuits and consequences of dispossession: The racialized realignment of the public sphere for U.S. youth. *Transforming Anthropology, 17*(1), 20-33.

Fine, M., Torre, M. E., Boudin, K., Bowen, I., Clark, J., Hylton, D., Martinez, M., 'Missy', Rivera, M., Roberts, R. A., Smart, P., & Upegui, D. (2003). Participatory action research: Within and beyond bars (pp. 173-198). In P. Camic, J. E. Rhodes, & L. Yardley (Eds.), *Qualitative research in psychology: Expanding perspectives in methodology and design*. Washington, DC: American Psychological Association.

Foth, M., & Adkins, B. (2006). A research design to build effective partnerships between city planners, developers, government and urban neighbourhood communities. *The Journal of Community Informatics, 2*(2). Retrieved from http://eprints.qut.edu.au/3677/1/3677_2.pdf

Greenbaum, J., & Loi, D. (2012). Participation, the camel and the elephant of design: An introduction. *CoDesign: International Journal of CoCreation in Design and the Arts, 8*(2-3), 81-85.

Glick, J. A. (1999). Focus groups in political campaigns. In D. D. Perlmutter (Ed.), *The Manship School guide to political communication* (pp. 114-121). Baton Rouge, LA: Louisiana State University Press.

Haraway, D. J. (1985). A cyborg manifesto: Science, technology, and socialist-feminism in the Late Twentieth Century. *Socialist Review, 80*, 65-108.

Harvey, D. (2010). *A companion to Marx's Capital*. New York, NY: Verso.

Hunter, D. (2003). Cyberspace as place and the tragedy of the digital anticommons. *California Law Review*, *91*(2), 439-519.

Katz, C. (1998). Whose nature, whose culture? In B. Braun & N. Castree (Eds.), *Remaking reality: Nature at the millennium* (pp. 46-63). London: Routledge.

Katz, C. (2004). *Growing up global: Economic restructuring and children's everyday lives.* Minneapolis, MIN: University of Minnesota Press.

Lenhart, A. (2012). *Teens, smartphones & texting.* Pew Internet & American Life Project. Retrieved from http://pewinternet.org/Reports/2012/Teens-and-smartphones.aspx

Lenhart, A., Madden, M., Smith, A., Purcell, K., Zickuhr, K., & Rainie, L. (2011). *Teens, kindness and cruelty on social network sites.* Pew Internet & American Life Project. Retrieved from http://pewinternet.org/Reports/2011/Teens-and-social-media.aspx

Low, S., Donovan, G. T., & Gieseking, J. (2012). Shoestring democracy: Gated condominiums and market-rate cooperatives in New York. *Journal of Urban Affairs*, *34*(3), 279-296.

Low, S. (2006). How private interests take over public space: Zoning, taxes, and incorporation of gated communities (pp. 81-104). In S. Low, & N. Smith (Eds.), *The politics of public space.* New York, NY: Routledge.

Luttrell, W. (2010). Interactive and reflexive models of qualitative research design. In W. Luttrell (Ed.), *Qualitative educational research: Readings in reflexive methodology and transformative practice* (pp. 159-164). New York, NY: Routledge.

McCarthy, J., & Wright, P. (2004). *Technology as experience.* Cambridge: MIT Press.

Mitchell, K., Marston, S. A., & Katz, C. (2003). Life's work: An introduction, review and critique. *Antipode*, *X*, 415-442.

Monahan, T. (2006). The surveillance curriculum: Risk management and social control in the neoliberal school (pp. 109-124). In T. Monahan (Ed.), *Surveillance and security: Technological politics and power in everyday life.* New York, NY: Routledge.

Nielsen Wire. (2011). *New mobile obsession: U.S. teens triple data usage.* Retrieved from http://blog.nielsen.com/nielsenwire/online_mobile/new-mobile-obsession-u-s-teens-triple-data-usage

Postman, N. (2000). The humanism of media ecology. *Proceedings of the Media Ecology Association, Volume 1.* Fordham University, New York, NY. Retrieved from http://www.media-ecology.org/publications/MEA_proceedings/v1/postman01.pdf

Saegert, S., Fields, D., & Libman, K. (2009). Deflating the dream: Radical risk and the neoliberalization of homeownership. *Journal of Urban Affairs*, *31*(3), 297-317.

Schuurman, N. (2004). Databases and bodies: A cyborg update. *Environment and Planning A, 36*, 1333-1340.

Smith, N. (1996). *New urban frontier: Gentrification and the revanchist city.* New York, NY: Routledge.

Gregory T. Donovan
Assistant Professor of Communication and Media Studies
Fordham University
USA

OVE EDVARD HATLEVIK AND GUNSTEIN EGEBERG

6. CHALLENGES ARISING WHEN USING FIELD NOTES AND VIDEO OBSERVATIONS

A Close Study of Teachers' Use of Interactive Whiteboards in a Norwegian School

INTRODUCTION

It is often useful for educational researchers to visit schools and follow teachers and pupils during lessons. However what is the role of the researchers when visiting schools? Are they supposed to be silent observers or to provide feedback to the schools? Feedback from researchers to teachers can have impact on and change teachers practice. This brings out some dilemmas. Firstly, how well are the data that underlie the researchers' analyses suited for giving advice and suggestions? Secondly, how are the teachers interpreting the feedback from the researchers? Thirdly, how are researchers capable to adequately manage both the role of the researcher and the advisor?

In this paper we are presenting and discussing experiences from a research project where researchers were asked to follow the implementation of Interactive whiteboards (IWBs) in a school. The research group, the school and the teachers had different goals and expectations of the outcome of the researchers' participation in the project. The researchers wanted to provide data to illuminate their research questions, while the school wanted to get feedback on the implementation of technology. The teachers on their hand wanted detailed feedback on their teaching with technology. These goals and expectations were not clearly defined or well discussed as the research project was launched.

When researchers act as pedagogical advisors providing recommendations for practical use of IWBs in the classroom, both academic professional and ethical issues arise. The researcher must be willing to analyse findings that are not necessarily relevant for their research questions, but that is relevant for the practitioner. Further, good and relevant feedback depends on quality of data, relevance of data and the researcher's ability to make sound judgements and to actually communicate their feedback to the teachers. In this chapter we are examining the role of the researcher when entering schools acting both as researchers and educational experts.

– What are the challenges that arise from using field notes and video recording in terms of achieving transparent and consistent analysis?
– What are important issues to consider when giving feedback, based on analysis of observation, to teachers?

G.B. Gudmundsdottir and K.B. Vasbø (Eds.), Methodological Challenges When Exploring Digital Learning Spaces in Education,79–94.

THEORETICAL PERSPECTIVES

Theoretical knowledge about various aspects of IWB use in schools is obviously important to be able to choose suitable methods, design proper research activities and perform valid analyses. To some extent we have discussed theory with the teachers, mainly during interviews and workshops. This section gives a brief overview over the theory used to support our research project.

Research on IWBs in Schools

An IWB is essentially a surface on which a computer screen is displayed, normally via a projector (Egeberg, Hatlevik, Wølner, Dalaaker, & Pettersen, 2011). The surface is sensitive to the touch, either by using a pen or finger, and lets the user control the computer from the board itself. During the last decade, IWBs for teaching purposes have been installed in schools worldwide (Egeberg & Hatlevik, 2012).

Guðmundsdóttir and Pettersen (2012) reviewed the international research literature on IWBs in education, which reported a relatively strong interest in research on IWBs from the beginning of the 2000s, and accordingly they found some 150 research papers, reports and theses of interest, reflecting a variety of themes linked to IWB. IWBs may be discussed in terms of understanding the technology, (teacher) training, school management, classroom management, motivation or learning outcomes. Guðmundsdóttir and Pettersen's review shows that there is a strong focus on the use of IWB in science, mathematics and languages, but less attention on the use of IWB in other subjects such as social studies, arts and crafts, music and the practical arts. The majority of the articles and reports relating to the IWB that Guðmundsdóttir and Pettersen (2012) found, featured a qualitative research approach.

It is essential to highlight three key findings from the literature review by Guðmundsdóttir and Pettersen (2012). First, with only a few exceptions (Lerman & Zevenbergen, 2007; Zevenbergen & Lerman, 2008), systematic studies that follow the use of IWBs in schools over a number of years are lacking. Second, there are few reported examples of schools or teachers who have implemented IWBs very successfully in teaching.

Implications for Practice with IWBs

Hennessy (2011) believes that IWBs can open and develop cooperation and dialogue in education, as they provide the opportunity to discuss issues from different perspectives. Educationists recognize the importance of students having a central role in classroom activities. This is something that IWBs can support (Beauchamp & Kennewell, 2009), because the students can be active by participating in dialogue with each other and with the teachers.

A common theme in the research literature points out that the successful use of IWBs depends on educational adaptation, classroom management and the ability of teachers to see the professional capabilities of IWBs in teaching (Mercer, Hennesey, & Warwick, 2010; Egeberg et al., 2011; Underwood & Dillon, 2011; Warwick & Mercer, 2011). However, several studies show that the school, teachers and students often have difficulty taking advantage of the anticipated pedagogical benefits of IWBs (Beauchamp & Parkinson, 2005; Egeberg & Wølner, 2011; Mercer, Warwick, Kershner, & Staarman, 2010; Wolfgang, Lauritzen, & Mortensen, 2011).

Hartley (2007) analysed the success stories about implementation of technology in schools, concluding that the implementation of IWBs requires good planning, sufficient time and the involvement of management, teachers, students and the technical staff. Littleton, Twiner, Gillen, Staarman and Mercer (2007) believe that IWBs provide enhanced opportunities for planning lessons, particularly in terms of organisation of learning activities.

Further, Gillen, Staarman, Littleton, Mercer and Twins (2012) conducted a series of classroom observations and teacher interviews and concluded that IWBs permitted better structuring of the lesson and raised the level of learning among all pupils (Gillen et al., 2012; Cuthell, 2005). Other recent studies have focused on whether and how information and communication technology (ICT) can help students in school (Mercer et al., 2010; Warwick, Hennessy, & Mercer, 2011), while Warwick and Kershner point out that ICT can help pupils at school provided there are teachers who control the learning environment through whole-class, teacher-led sessions (Harlow, Cowie, & Heazlewood, 2010; Harlow, Taylor, & Forret, 2011; Warwick & Kershner, 2008).

With some of these issues in mind it is interesting to reflect upon how teachers change their teaching when they use an IWB. It seems that teachers are inclined to use it as a support tool for management and control as opposed to a pedagogical tool. Thus, an IWB does not automatically lead to significant changes in a teacher's pedagogical approach, something that might be imagined and desired (Avidov-Ungar & Eshete-Alkakay, 2011; Underwood & Dillon, 2011). However, the expectation that teachers change their practice rather than adapt their use of the IWB to existing practice may be unrealistic.

Winzenried, Dalgarno and Tinkler (2010) argue that an IWB can be used without any training. However, there are studies that show that teachers and schools are experiencing technical problems with IWBs (Bal, Misirli, Orhan, Yucel, & Sarin, 2010; DeSantis, 2012; Warwick & Kershner, 2008). Therefore, experts stress the need to ensure adequate training for teachers and school administrators (Glover & Miller, 2007, 2009). Specifically, teachers need subject-related training in the use of IWBs (Egeberg & Hatlevik, 2012).

Winter, Winterbottom and Wilson (2010) interviewed students in England to examine their experience with the use of new technology in science. They too found that, in order to achieve the educational benefits of technology, it is necessary to support the teachers. DeSantis (2012) sets out the following conditions for implementing IWBs in schools. First, the teachers need instruction and training in order to facilitate their use of IWBs. Second, there must be long-term cooperative relationships among teaching staff. Third, teachers and students should be monitored to encourage active use of the IWBs.

Video Analysis and Change in Teachers' Practise

Following the technological development in video capture equipment there has been an increasing interest for using video as a tool for developing teachers' practise (Seidel, Stürmer, Bloomberg, Kobarg, & Schwindt, 2011; Tripp & Rich, 2012). Today's cameras are small, relatively cheap and easy to use. Software has equally dropped in price and offers more functionality in interfaces that is steadily getting easier to operate.

There are numerous research papers on the use of video in teacher training, but as Seidel and colleagues discuss there are few projects, which study *the actual change* in teacher practise when using video analysis (Seidel et al., 2011). As for empirical data, reports are based various kinds of video material, either of the teacher's own practise or that of others. In the last category you will find both video of known colleagues and more general instructional resources. Several reports (Seidel et al., 2011; Tripp & Rich, 2012) utilize combinations of these types of video sources. Teachers tend to value video of their own practise more than that of others.

Recent reports document how the use of video analysis in teacher training (either as pre service or as continuous professional development) might impact on teacher practise. Seidel et al. (2011) documented how the use of video analysis improved teachers' knowledge-based reasoning and that it activated prior knowledge, Tripp and Rich (2012) found that video analysis aided their change process through all four phases: recognition the need for change, brainstorming for ideas, implementing change ideas and evaluating the changes that were implemented. Teachers report various benefits when using video in analysing their practise. Zhang, Wang and Kolodinsky (2010) found that teachers value the possibility to get a window into their practise, and that they found the videos to be objective. Objectiveness is on the other hand easy to overrate, Roschelle (2000) points out four issues in this case: The camera does not capture the same as the human eye, the camera has a point of view, not all (sometimes even very little) context is captured and a research video is not the same as a research paper.

According to Zhang et al. (2010) teachers emphasize the importance of both individual and collective reflections; the video material used in their research, published videos, colleagues' videos and videos of own practise, supported both types.

THE RESEARCH CASE

The origin of the data is a research project involving one school on its way of implementing IWBs. The school has 70 staff members and 550 pupils from 1st to 10th grade. According to the school's strategy, forums and seminars for students are among the preferred teaching strategies. The school has a library and the school librarian has a teaching role, i.e. instructing students how to search for information.

In particular, the school wanted to focus on the 7th grade and the use of IWBs in Norwegian and mathematics. The intention of choosing 7th grade and these subjects was following and comparing their experience with a Nordic IWB project (Wolfgang, Lauritzen, & Mortensen, 2011). The three teachers at the 7th grade level did not have much experience with IWB prior to the project, but were asked by the school management to participate. The three teachers were invited to participate in an external qualifying IWB course at a local college in order to empower them to deal with the new demands of IWBs.

In the period from autumn 2010 to spring 2011, three research groups joined forces and followed the 7th grade teachers as they started to use IWBs (Egeberg et al., 2011; Egeberg & Wølner, 2011). Researchers from the University Colleges in Vestfold and Buskerud, together with researchers from the Norwegian Centre for ICT in Education, investigate several issues related to 1. Assessment for learning, 2. Communication, 3. Classroom management with IWBs and 4. Didactic design.

The initial data collection was undertaken using classroom observations with video recordings combined with two observation forms – one open and one predefined. In addition interviews were conducted with both students and teachers. Even a short student survey was administered. In depth descriptions of these instruments can be found in the final report of the project (Egeberg & Wølner, 2011). The school leadership and the three teachers participating in the study expected to receive feedback from the researchers on the four topics mentioned above, along with recommendations on the implementation of IWBs. Therefore, three workshops for teachers and researchers were organized during the research period. The experiences from these workshops were documented in short commentary notes. The main subjects for the study were Norwegian and mathematics; these two core subjects are equally emphasized.

The qualitative methods included classroom observations from 19 lessons in mainly Norwegian and mathematic classes. Furthermore, two well-planned focus group interviews were conducted, one in the early phase and one in the conclusive. Also students were interviewed, two different groups, one early and one late in the project. Each of the interviews lasted about 60 minutes. The interviews were captured through the use of audio and notes for the teachers, and video and notes for the students. Video was chosen for the latter as this would make it easier to identify each student. In addition to this there have been many informal and undocumented talks with both students and teachers.

As for quantitative data two approaches were chosen. The students were exposed to a questionnaire, with 49 questions, about their perception of the use of IWB in terms of motivation, learning, technical mastery, but also about frequencies of use and level of noise. Social-economic background was also included. The other approach involved analysing the structured field notes with the aim of identifying tendencies in classroom activity when IWBs are in use. Since the quantitative data did not play an important role in the problems we discuss here, these data are not discussed further.

The project aimed to find examples of and experiences with the use of interactive whiteboards (IWBs). Validity of the study depends on attaining transparency in the observations and achieving consistent analysis both within and between the research groups and with the teachers.

METHOD

As Beauchamp (2004, p. 329) has indicated, data collection, validation, interpretation and action are four stages of the fieldwork process. Section 4 is organized according to Beauchamp's framework.

Data Collection

This study draws mainly on data collected from teacher interviews and notes taken from teacher workshops. However, experiences and reflections around the methods used in the research case go beyond what is collected in the interviews and notes, they are hands on experiences and act as a part of the authors' underlying knowledge in this case.

Interviews
Three one-hour long interviews were conducted with teachers (autumn 2010, spring 2011 and autumn 2012). The first two interviews were part of the research project described above, while the latter was part of a follow-up study for a later project (Egeberg & Hatlevik, 2012). Even though the interviews had slightly different scopes, they all revolved around the three teachers' experiences with the use of IWBs in planning and actual teaching. The interviews were semi-structured, but as mentioned, not standardized. The interviews give insight in a variety of issues concerning the teachers practice, but most important in this case is the value they have as documentation of change and development.

Notes from workshops
From the already described workshops notes were taken. These notes are a mixture of concrete actions having taken place, and immediate reflections made by the researchers. Even though the notes were not very extensive, they still gave a lot of valuable input about the discussions taking place during the sessions.

Data collection was reported to and approved by the Norwegian Social Science Data Services (NSD) in relation to the observations during 2010/2011 and for the interviews in 2012.

Validation

The study concerned three teachers using IWBs while delivering Norwegian and mathematics lessons in two classes of pupils in the 7th grade. The teachers were recruited to a project described in the section on "The Research Case". Three interviews were conducted, all of about one hour's duration. The interviews were in all cases lead by two researchers to increase validity. Notes were taken, but the primary data capture method was in all three cases video. Video was then transcribed using the software InqScribe version 2.1.

As mentioned there were held three teacher workshops. Notes were taken from these workshops, mostly in a not too structured manner. The notes include information about action points and minutes from the discussions, but also some reflections made by either teachers or researchers. All notes are analysed by more than one researcher.

Findings from both data sources have been thoroughly analysed by both authors of this report.

Interpretation of the Methods Used in the Research Case

Data in the research case were collected through the use of observation notes and video recordings. As in other studies on IWBs in classrooms some observations went on for shorter periods of time (Beauchamp, 2004; Glover & Miller, 2009; Mercer, Hennessy, & Warwick, 2010; Schuck & Kearney, 2007) and others for longer (Lerman & Zevenbergen, 2007; Zevenbergen & Lerman, 2008).

Two types of observation forms were used. One observation form contained predefined categories based on an operationalization of the research questions for the study (quantitative data). The purpose of this was to obtain an idea of what was going on and which activities predominated during the teaching sessions (Kleven & Strømsnes, 1998). The disadvantages of a form with predefined categories are that the observer may be influenced by assumptions that he or she brings into the classroom, and thus it may be difficult to capture interesting events that do not fit directly into the predefined categories. The other observation form was therefore more open-ended and could be used specifically for recording something interesting or unexpected (qualitative data). The activities recorded were time-coded, before being briefly described and presented to the other researchers involved in the project. Time data could be used to link notes from this form to the video recordings, supplementary notes or the more structured observation form.

Two types of video recordings were used. Initially, we placed a camera at the back of the classroom pointing towards the IWB, thus capturing the teacher's face but only the backs of the pupils. This was appropriate for whole-class teaching, although it was difficult to record interactions between teachers and pupils using only one camera. In both the Norwegian and mathematics lessons, pupils had the opportunity to solve problems while standing by the IWB. Typically, groups of pupils were sent to the IWB to undertake a particular task introduced by the teacher. Again, the positioning of the camera at the back of the classroom proved unsuitable, so after having reviewed the first video recordings we decided to move it forward, closer to the activities and interactions that took place in front of the IWB. In some cases we used two cameras in the classroom, the second would then either be stationary placed in the front of the classroom, or used handheld focusing on the IWB activity. Further reviews of these approaches concluded that the handheld camera, or a stationary placed close to the IWB, provided the best data.

Between 60 and 70% of the activities during a normal lesson were based on prepared teaching material, solving problems or summarising points.

Overall, the emergence of researchers with notebooks and video camera can have impact on the students', teachers' and researchers' behaviour. Furthermore, video-aided reflections on practise have the power to change teacher behaviour, a well-known fact (Borg, Kallenbach, Morris, & Friebel, 1969; Kleinknecht & Schneider, 2013). The professional development method of *Microteaching* builds upon this fact, here video is used in structured analysis of teacher practise. For the researcher many questions arise when using video (Roschelle, 2000):

– Use of video has limitations. The video captures less than the human eye, the video has a certain point of view and is sensible to placement. Furthermore, video captures only part of the context, especially when it comes to activities that occur over time. Video material can be analysed through a variety of methods, showing video to others might easily result in new analysis.

– When presenting video data careful thinking is necessary. Which cases does one choose; i.e. the best one or the most common one? Are the criteria for choosing clips known and discussed? And how much context do you include? More contexts often result in longer clips.

Ultimately, it might be appropriate to produce a promotional video to help disseminate results (Roschelle, 2000). Such a video will in itself need careful planning.

Action: Descriptions from the Research Case

One aim of the observations was to identify the activities that took place in the classroom. When observers were using the observation forms, they were also analysing what they saw and taking notes. The open field forms included a heading, a time and a brief description of what was observed. Analysis of the open forms was based on the theme or topic described in the form. The structured observation form contained descriptions of when and how often an activity happened. This information could be quantified and summarised to describe trends and patterns in the activities that took place during the lesson. Additionally, combinations of these two types of notes could be used to study patterns in the predefined observation forms in more detail. However, as the analyses were undertaken at the same time as the data collection, it could be difficult to get an overall perspective of what was happening in the classroom.

The purpose of the video observation was to allow analysis of classroom activities, whether in full lessons or in shorter sequences, to be conducted after the observations had taken place. Observation notes could also be used in conjunction with the video to refer back to activities that stood out as interesting, unexpected or relevant to the research questions. In order to analyse the data obtained from video observations, the software tool InqScribe was used to transcribe all recorded observations. This tool makes it possible to enter codes, comments and analyses of events, tasks and isolated statements. The video footage was analysed to find examples of activities and discussions related to the research questions of the project, namely examples of teaching practice with IWBs.

FOUR STRATEGIES FOR CAPTURING PRACTICE IN THE CLASSROOM

This section describes four different approaches to capture what took place in the classrooms during the project case study. Two are related to the use of video data, the other two related to the use of the observation forms.

Approach A: Video Recording – Whole Classroom

We placed a video camera on a tripod at the back of the classroom facing the teacher and the IWB. The recording started at the beginning of the lesson and continued until the end.

The advantage of using a video camera was that it was possible to review and discuss the whole or parts of the material with other people, to share the material and to subject it to detailed analysis. In case of disagreement or uncertainty, it is always possible to go back to the taped raw data.

The disadvantages of using video observation are that it takes considerable time to watch and to review the material. It also takes time to transcribe and analyse the data. Further, in our study, the placement of the camera at the back of the classroom made it difficult for researchers to understand the speech and to identify the pupils who were speaking, especially those who talked in a soft voice.

However, the videos could be used as the basis for discussions with the teachers; although it took some time before analyses of findings and appropriate video clips could be submitted for the teachers' comment. It also took time to play and discuss the recording with teachers. Finally, it is possible that the video clips were perceived as a "whole truth" status, something that was not intended by the researchers. As mentioned, video data have limitations.

Overall, whole-class teaching took up 40-50% of the time. The video of the teachers' whole-class activities could, in theory, be analysed and presented to them during the workshops. In practice, however, these video clips were not shown or discussed in the teacher-researcher workshops.

Approach B: Close-Up Video Recording – Pupils by the IWB

In both Norwegian and mathematics, the teachers normally started each lesson with whole-class teaching and then let the pupils work on their own or in groups on tasks the teacher gave them. A static camera proved not to be a good way to capture class activities when pupils worked on their own or with others. In activities like this you really need to get up close to capture the details of the activities. The research teams therefore decided to move the camera forward to the IWB to video the pupils working there. The camera was placed to one side of the

IWB, and in this way we got video data of the IWB and the pupils standing in front of it.

One advantage of close-up videotaping was that the quality of speech and pictures were greatly improved, making it possible to identify the pupil speaking and what the pupils were doing and saying.

However, as with whole-class video recording, it was time consuming to transcribe the recordings and to identify and keep track of pupils' voices and activities. Close-up videoing was unable to document what the rest of the class were doing while a small group was working by the IWB. Moreover, we discovered that working in groups constituted a small portion of the lessons.

In the workshops, several examples of pupils at the IWB were presented and discussed by the researchers and teachers. They included: recordings of a single student working on his own by the IWB, groups of students answering quiz questions and students working with fractions in mathematics. These three examples profited on the transparent data from both video recording and transcriptions. Moreover, the videos enabled participants to debate and arrive at conclusions about what they did and did not agree on and to assess the consistency of their findings.

Approach C: Structured Observation Form

A structured observation form for activities in the classroom was developed for the project. The form was used in lessons in both Norwegian and mathematics. The structured observation form consisted of two main dimensions: time and activities. A record was made every third minute of activity in the class.

The advantage of the structured observation form was the ability to provide the teachers with instant feedback. The form contained descriptive information, but not very specific feedback about how the teachers were teaching. For example, although the form recorded whether the teacher was talking or the students were asking questions, it did not contain any data about the *quality* of these activities. Another disadvantage of the form was that it contained predefined categories based on an understanding of the research questions. Accordingly, it was not easy to document interesting events that did not fit the format of the form. Finally, when using the structured observation form, analysis occurred simultaneously with data collection, requiring concentration, the ability to interpret the situation and perception of the categories. This was a possible source of error of interpretation or failure to follow what was happening.

After its first use in the two classrooms, a discussion took place between the researchers about how to understand the various categories on the form, e.g. what might be described as *dialogue* and how this differed from *question and answer*. Although it is possible to compare different people's observations, this does require that the observers have synchronised the timing of when to enter observations. Furthermore, a need may emerge, based on the observation experiences, to designate several further categories or subcategories, reflecting different dimensions of an activity such as open questions and closed questions.

Overall, the structured form enabled certain characteristics of the lesson to be identified. It also permitted comparison of teaching in the subjects of Norwegian and mathematics, revealing similarities and differences. However, different observers may have understood terms differently, leading to uncertainty about the results. It was also difficult to be specific about what teachers did and said during the course of an hour, which in turn easily could influence the accuracy of the form data.

Analyses from these structured field notes were used in a workshop in the spring of 2011. The observations were summarised, showing the use of IWBs in Norwegian and mathematics. However, these analyses were mainly descriptive, and it was difficult to apply them in the form of recommendations to the teachers.

Approach D: Supplementary Notes

In conjunction with the observations, we chose to use a simple template for supplementary notes to record interesting events, both events that related directly to the research questions and those that went beyond the themes in the research questions. Such notes were used in conjunction with the structured observation form and the video recordings.

The field notes form was a sheet divided into three parts to record time of observation (the times being intended to align with the video recordings and the observation forms), a heading and a description of the findings.

The notes were focused on main themes, which allowed them to be quickly read through at the end of a lesson and compared with the other material for closer study (as the times were aligned).

The field notes form was supposed to be used in all of the lessons observed during the research period of 2010/11. However, only a few forms were actually filled out. The observer often had to address issues with the technology (video/audio), something that made observation difficult. Furthermore there was a lack of common understanding of the function of the open-ended form. As the purpose was unclear, the observer was uncertain about what to put in the form. Therefore they did not on their own provide enough information for analysis.

The supplementary notes form also had other drawbacks. First, they required that the observers perform initial analysis of events during the lesson, which demanded attention. Less attention could then be directed at capturing what was going on in the classroom. Second, they contained only brief descriptions of each observation point, thus missing contextual data and more in-depth analysis. Moreover, it was not possible to go back to the raw data for verification in case of differences of interpretation.

In light of some of these difficulties, the supplementary notes were never used in the workshops or in discussions with teachers. They ended up being used, to a limited extent, in getting an overview of the data in the explorative early phase of the analysis, but never as a stand-alone data source.

DISCUSSION

What are the challenges of using field notes and video recording when it comes to achieving transparent and consistent analyses? Close-up video and whole-class video recordings showed both differences and similarities in the data analysis.

Overall, video recordings provided raw data, to which the researchers could return for verification and analysis. Both data and analyses thus afforded transparency for researchers and teachers involved in the project. However, it is undoubtedly time consuming to view the videos, transcribe them and read through the transcriptions. It is possible to examine the degree of consistency between those who review and analyse video, but this depends on how the selection and discussion of the examples are organised. It is seldom possible to present all the material, and therefore selections have to be made. Which selections should be made and presented?

An advantage of taking notes is that they permit a fairly quick overview of the situation or reveal trends, but they may not bring out more subtle or hidden characteristics of a situation. The data contained in notes are not so transparent, because the observation includes analysis, which involves processing and elaboration of the facts.

Finally, what are the challenges with regard to providing feedback to teachers? The teachers would not consent to participate in a study in which researchers come and go without providing some feedback. A school leader emphasised the need for researchers to give feedback so that the school would derive immediate benefit from participating in the project.

The notes taken by researchers served as a basis for discussion and reflection just after the lesson. Video recordings, on the other hand, were a source of deeper and more detailed feedback for teachers. The close-up video recordings in particular provided more detailed and specific information than the whole-class recordings, by documenting an excerpt of what happened in the lesson; thereby, however, it necessarily suffered from the disadvantage of focusing on only a small portion of the lesson.

The activities, in which pupils interacted with each other, though important, constituted only a minor portion of each lesson. It is therefore a paradox that the researchers, in providing feedback to teachers, put the most emphasis on activities that made up the least amount of time. By contrast, no feedback was given on what the teacher did when, for example, presenting assignments on the IWB. The rather autonomous Norwegian teacher makes his or hers choices when planning and delivering teaching as a result of their professional knowledge (Carlgren & Klette, 2008). It is often challenging for the researcher to comment on all sides of the teacher's practise, something that in turn obviously would influence on which aspects the researchers would emphasize in their analysis. As a result, while the researchers were focusing on how the pupils were dealing with the IWBs and making this a main focus in the analysis, this was a less central activity for the teacher.

Teachers were incorporating the use of the interactive boards into their lesson plans, as they felt the IWBs had an advantage over traditional blackboards. The workshops with the teachers, however, did not concentrate on activities in whole-class teaching, yet this constituted the largest part of most lessons and it was this that teachers were planning for. Hence, there was a disparity between the focus of the teachers and that of the researchers giving feedback to them. Whereas the researchers were interested in the teachers' perspectives in the hope of arriving at consistent conclusions, the teachers tended to be more interested in practical implications. A video clip might be used as a tool for researchers achieving consensus when concluding on empirical findings, but a teacher might view the clip with another intention: Improving his or hers practise.

CONCLUDING REMARKS

There are several challenges in applying different ways of observation. Indeed, it may not be possible to illuminate the same phenomenon through different observation approaches. Rather, light may be shed on different phenomena or aspects of the topic.

In the context of the present research, video recording yielded transparent data and potentially consistent findings and analyses. This does not preclude the use of notes, which gave an overview of a situation and can be a strong indicator in choosing which sequences to prioritise for transcription and analysis.

A further challenge in this research is how to produce feedback that is useful for teachers and schools. There is probably no single research method that is guaranteed to yield relevant feedback. It may be that researchers have skills appropriate to conducting research but lack the expertise to know what the relevant issues are for teachers.

It is undoubtedly important to carry out research with a critical perspective on technology; however, in talking to teachers, it is also necessary to offer suggestions and alternative ways of teaching or organising learning activities. Teachers need to receive both critical and constructive input on their teaching.. Nevertheless, one might ask what is the appropriate forum for the organisation of feedback to teachers? Is a workshop in which researchers discuss and dispute their findings the right setting or would another type of feedback give better results? Ethical dilemmas are always eminent, when looking back it is clear that some of the choices made by the researchers gave an unwanted result. Most striking is how the video scenes presented to the teachers as a basis for deep reflection and discussion actually turned out. From the researchers' perspective the chosen scenes were concrete and to a large extent concerned with two aspects of teaching with IWBs: the fact that using software intended for individual use often will provide little possibility for high quality group processes and also for the care the teacher needs to take to compose well-functioning student groups. These two main points were of interest for the researcher, but it turned out that the teachers might have seen these scenes differently, and that the teachers might have perceived the following discussion as a form of criticism. This again might have led to the fact that the

91

teachers abolished the use of IWBs in student oriented learning situations. It is a danger that the researchers, with their very best intentions, have influenced the teachers in such a way that their use of IWBs might have ended up being of a lesser value in student based activities. If so, one of the important factors emphasized by IWB researcher is gone.

This research case study of the introduction of IWBs tried both to answer distinct research questions and to provide feedback to teachers about practical solutions to the challenges of using the IWB. The study attempts to cover many topics related to the use of IWBs. It is also a project with multiple participating institutions and researchers. It is therefore necessary to allow all the participants to go through and make their own interpretations of the video recordings and the transcripts. Further, giving feedback to teachers on their teaching practice requires educational and technological expertise from the researchers. This indicates a need to design research groups that possess the necessary knowledge and experience to achieve the goals of the study and at the same time meet the expectations of the participating teachers.

REFERENCES

Avidov-Ungar, O., & Eshet- Alkakay, Y. (2011). Teachers in a world of change: Teachers' knowledge and attitudes towards the implementation of innovative technologies in schools. *Interdisciplinary Journal of E-Learning and Learning Objects, 7,* 291-303.

Bal, G., Misirli, G., Orhan, N., Yucel, K., & Sarin, Y. G. (2010, June). *Teachers' expectations from computer technology and interactive whiteboard: A survey.* Paper presented at the International Conference on Education Technology and Computer Conference (ICETC), China.

Beauchamp, G. (2004). Teacher use of the interactive whiteboard in primary schools: Towards an effective transition framework. *Technology, Pedagogy and Education, 13,* 327-348.

Beauchamp, G., & Kennewell, S. (2009). Interactivity in the classroom and its impact on learning. *Computers & Education, 54,* 759-766.

Beauchamp, G., & Parkinson, J. (2005). Beyond the 'wow' factor: Developing interactivity with the interactive whiteboard. *School Science Review, 86,* 97-104.

Borg, W. R., Kallenbach, W., Morris, M., & Friebel, A. (1969). Videotape feedback and microteaching in a teacher training. *The Journal of Experimental Education, 37*(4), 9-16.

Carlgren, I., & Klette, K. (2008). Reconstructions of Nordic teachers: Reform policies and teachers' work during the 1990s. *Scandinavian Journal of Educational Research, 52,* 117-133.

Cuthell, J. P. (2005). The impact of interactive whiteboards on teaching, learning and attainment. In J. Price, D. Willis, N. Davis, & J. Willis (Eds.), *Proceedings of SITE 2005* (pp. 1353-1355). Norfolk, VA: Association for the Advancement of Computing in Education.

Cresswell, J. W. (2003). *Research design: Qualitative, quantitative, and mixed methods approaches.* London: Sage Publications Ltd.

DeSantis, J. (2012). Getting the most from your interactive whiteboard investment: Three guiding principles for designing effective professional development. *The Clearing House: A Journal of Educational Strategies, Issues and Ideas, 85*(2), 51-55.

Egeberg, G., & Hatlevik, O. E. (2012). Erfaringer og forventninger: Læreres refleksjoner over bruk av interaktive tavler [Experiences and expectations: Teachers' reflections on the use of interactive whiteboards]. In D. Dalaaker et al., *Kvalitativ monitor 2012* [Qualitative monitor 2012]. Oslo: Senter for IKT i utdanningen.

Egeberg, G., & Wølner, T. A. (2011). *"Board or bored". The final report.* Oslo: Senter for IKT i utdanningen.

Egeberg, G., Hatlevik, O. E., Wølner, T. A, Dalaaker, D., & Pettersen, G. O. (2011). *"Board or bored? – A Nordic collaborative project on interactive whiteboards.* Oslo: Senter for IKT i utdanningen.

Gillen, J., Littleton, K., Twiner, A., Staarman, J. K., & Mercer, N. (2012). A learning revolution? Investigating pedagogic practice around interactive whiteboards in British primary classrooms. *Learning Media and Technology, 32,* 243-256.

Glover, D., & Miller, D. (2007). Leading changed classroom culture – The impact of interactive whiteboards. *British Educational Leadership, Management & Administration Society, 21,* 21-24.

Glover, D., & Miller, D. (2009). Optimising the use of interactive whiteboards: An application of developmental work research in the United Kingdom. *Professional Development in Education, 35,* 469-483.

Guðmundsdóttir, G. B., & Pettersen, S. (2012). Hva forteller eksisterende forskning om bruk av interaktive tavler? [What does existing research on the use of interactive whiteboards show?]. In D. Dalaaker et al., *Kvalitativ monitor 2012* [Qualitative monitor 2012]. Oslo: Senter for IKT i utdanningen.

Harlow, A., Cowie, B., & Heazlewood. M. (2010). Keeping in touch with learning: The use of interactive whiteboard in the junior school. *Teachnology, Pedagogy and Education, 19,* 237-243.

Harlow, A., Taylor, M., & Forret, M. (2011). Using an interactive whiteboard and a computer-programming tool to support the development of the key competencies in the New Zealand curriculum. *Computers in New Zealand Schools: Learning, teaching, technology, 23*(1), 101-107.

Hartley, J. (2007). Teaching, learning and new technology: A review for teachers. *British Journal of Educational Technology, 38,* 42-62.

Hennessy, S. (2011). The role of digital artefacts on the interactive whiteboard in supporting classroom dialogue. *Journal of Computer Assisted Learning, 27,* 463-489.

Kleinknecht , M., & Schneider, J. (2013). What do teachers think and feel when analyzing videos of themselves and other teachers teaching? *Teaching and Teacher Education 33,* 13-23.

Kleven, T. A., & Strømsnes, T. Å. (1998). Systematisk observasjon som tilnærming til klasseromsforskning [Systematic observation that approach to classroom research]. In K. Klette (Ed.), *Klasseromsforskning på norsk* [Classroom research in Norwegian] (pp. 35-56). Oslo: Ad Notam Forlag

Littleton, K., Twiner, A., Gillen, J., Staarman, J. K., & Mercer, N. (2007, August-September). *Orchestration with the Interactive Whiteboard.* Paper presented at EARLI 2007 Conference, Budapest, Hungary. Retrieved from http://oro.open.ac.uk/15279/2/earli_august_22ndho.pdf

Mercer, N., Warvick, P., Kershner, R., & Staarman, J. K. (2010). Can the interactive whiteboard help to provide 'dialogic space' for children's collaborative activity? *Language and Education, 24*(5), 367-384.

Mercer, N. Hennesey, S., & Warwick, P. (2010). Using interactive whiteboards to orchestrate classroom dialogue. *Technology, Pedagogy and Education, 19*(2), 195-209.

Roschelle, J. (2000). Choosing and using video equipment for data collection. In R. Lesh & A. Kelly (Eds.), *Handbook of research design in mathematics & science education* (pp. 457-486). Mahwah, NJ : Lawrence Erlbaum Associates, Inc.

Schuck, S., & Kearney, M. (2007). *Exploring pedagogy with interactive whiteboards: A research report.* Sydney: UTS. Retrieved from http://www.ed-dev.uts.edu.au/teachered/research/iwbproject/home.html.

Seidel, T., Stürmer, K., Bloomberg, G., Kobarg, M., & Schwindt, K. (2011). Teacher learning from analysis of videotaped classroom situations: Does it make a difference whether teachers observe their own teaching or that of others? *Teaching and Teacher Education, 27,* 259-267.

Tripp, T., & Rich, P. (2012). Using video to analyze one's own teaching. *British Journal of Educational Technology, 40,* 768-704.

Underwood, J., & Dillon, G. (2011). Chasing dreams and recognising realities: Teachers' responses to ICT. *Technology, Pedagogy and Education, 20,* 317-330.

Warvick, P., & Kershner, R. (2010). Primary teachers' understanding of the interactive whiteboard as a tool for children's collaborative learning and knowledge building. *Learning, Media & Technology, 33,* 269-287.

Warwick, P., & Mercer, N. (2011, September). *Using the interactive whiteboard to scaffold pupils' learning of science in collaborative group activity.* Paper presented at the EARLI 2011 Conference, University of Exeter. Retrieved from http://iwbcollaboration.educ.cam.ac.uk/publications/Scaffolding-symposium-paper-for-website.pdf.

Warwick, P., Hennessy, S., & Mercer, N. (2011). Promoting teacher and school development through co-enquiry: Developing interactive whiteboard use in a 'dialogic classroom'. *Teachers and Teaching, 17,* 303-324.

Winter, J. d., Winterbottom, M., & Wilson, E. (2010). Developing a user guide to integrating new technologies in science teaching and learning: Teachers' and pupils' perceptions of their affordances. *Technology, Pedagogy and Education, 19,* 261-267.

Winzenried, A., Dalgarno, B., & Tinkler, J. (2010). The interactive whiteboard: A transitional technology supporting diverse teaching practices. *Australasian Journal of Educational Technology, 26,* 534-552.

Wolfgang, C., Lauritzen, J., & Mortensen, S. (2011). *IT-integration i fagene – et brugerdrevent innovationsprojekt mellem Absalons Skole i Roskilde og University College Sjælland. Nordic SMART School Project.* Roskilde: University College Sjælland.

Yin, R.K. (1994). *Case study research: Design and methods* (2nd edition). London: Sage Publications.

Zevenbergen, R., & Lerman, S. (2007). Interactive whiteboards as mediating tools for teaching mathematics: Rhetoric or reality? In J-H. Woo, H-C. Lew, K-S. Park, & D-Y. Seo (Eds.), *Proceedings of the Thirty-First Meeting of the International Group for the Psychology of Mathematics Education* (Vol. 3 pp. 169-176). The Korea Society of Educational Studies in Mathematics.

Zevenbergen, R., & Lerman, S. (2008). Learning environments using interactive whiteboards: New learning spaces or reproduction of old technologies? *Mathematics Education Research Journal, 20*(1), 108-126.

Zhang, G., Wang, Q., & Kolodinsky, J. (2010). The digital divide in Internet information searching: A double-hurdle model analysis of household data from Vermont. *First Monday, 15,* 11-1.

Ove E. Hatlevik
Department of Technology and Analysis
The Norwegian Centre for ICT in Education
Norway

Gunstein Egeberg
Department of Education
The Arctic University of Norway
Norway

PART III

CHALLENGES WHEN EXPLORING CHILDREN'S MEANING MAKING IN DIGITAL CONTEXTS

TAMARA PRIBIŠEV BELESLIN

7. DIGITAL EXPERIENCES IN EARLY CHILDHOOD

Researching Emerging Perspectives, Ideas, Practices and Cultures

INTRODUCTION

In this chapter I will present the studies I have done in the past decade, as the empirical basis for understanding the digital culture and practices of young children in the *local context*. Relying upon several methods of inquiry and by putting different studies together in the spirit of a mixed research approach, this chapter re-composes *a mosaic* of understanding of children's digital experiences.

The main focus of the chapter is an inquiry into the methodological challenges arising from the same phenomenon during the period of ongoing paradigmatic changes. By representing three studies, the titles and basic characteristics are summarized in Table 1, I highlight the specific challenges and theoretical and methodological knowledge I acquired while working with each project. I have given each study a symbolic form as *pieces* of the mosaic, pointing to the possibility of their ambiguous readings and interpretations. Linearly and chronologically, the chapter shows three studies that longitudinally experienced shifts from simple to complex forms, which were connected with waves of development with regard to the social and theoretical ideas about young children and their technology use. I am representing the main results of these three studies in a visual language (Figures 1 and 2), as well as the many challenges and lessons that I have encountered. Further, the chapter can also be read as an interplay between different pieces of texts and pictures that portray a social phenomenon in a context, whose characteristics and dimensions highlight the multiple of layers comprised within it.

Studies were undertaken within a social and academic as well as a pedagogical community where there are no clearly articulated goals in relation to the digital practice and culture of contemporary young children. Likewise, there is no socially validated understanding of early digital literacy as social practice and necessary symbolic tools for living within a computer culture in a networked society. Yet, the studies indicated to the fact that such practice significantly shapes the childhood of a young child. Growing up immersed in such a semi-analogue, semi-digital context, superficially grasping reality (Pribišev Beleslin, 2011), children are still developing themselves in an *ad hoc* manner, forming their points of view, behaviours, and subcultures. This, among other things, supports the thesis that young children, as competent users of digital technologies, are participants in their

G.B. Gudmundsdottir and K.B. Vasbø (Eds.), Methodological Challenges When Exploring Digital Learning Spaces in Education, 97–113.

Table 1. A pathway to overview the studies

Study title	Perspectives / Kinds of research (Hatch, 2002)	Participants	Problem / Research focus	Data collection	Data analyses	Ethical considerations
The impact of ICT experiences on pre-school children's development (2008)	Positivist Ex-post-facto approach Explorative and co-relational study design survey	Teachers' assessment of the developmental indicators of 470 children from four- to six-years-old the in the capital of the Republic of Srpska (RS) Parents' assessment of children's experiences of computer use in the home (58.91% computer non-users, 41.09% computer users)	Impact of computer experiences on young children's development Positive effects and risks of computer activities in an informal environment (home)	Questionnaire for parents on children's computer experiences Questionnaire for teachers for assessment of indicators of development	MANOVA, discriminative analyses Roy's test, Pearson's coefficient of contingence (c), coefficient of multiple correlation (R) Cluster analyses	Parental agreement Personal data coding
"Listening" to children's drawings about their computer experiences (2007)	Post-positivist Artifact study	117 drawings by four- to five-year-olds	Insight into how a child creates meanings and "personal worlds" around digital experiences	Instrument for children's drawing	Open coding Comparison on similarities and differences in categories	Parental agreement Personal data coding
Growing up digitally (2012)	Constructivist Multi-method approach Play-based focus group Artifact study	10 focus groups with 59 five-year-olds 59 children's photographs of places in kindergarten 874 drawings by four- to five-year-olds throughout RS (80.66% non-users, 14.3% computer users, 5.03% missing data) Comments on what they have drawn	Listening to children's stories, collective constructs and understandings on growing up digitally as their everyday practice	Semi-structured group interviews with a doll as a researcher Instruments for children's drawing with comments Photographing while collecting the research documentation	Qualitative inductive analyses Visual data analyses	Consent of Ombudsman for children in RS Informing the parents Parental agreement Personal data coding Researcher's reflexivity Children could leave the research

own digital development, actively involved in community changes on various contextual levels.

In addition, the qualitative research paradigm has only recently received academic verification and application in the academic and professional community I come from. So, my frame of inquiry for this phenomenon has been formed by a limited body of knowledge and local understanding on the digital practices of young children, a lack of institutional practice in the application of digital technologies, the unavailability of many tools for researchers, such as databases, online libraries, contemporary periodicals, adequate funds and the like. It is also influenced through dialogue with a huge body of knowledge from different cultural, social and pedagogical contexts, which often, cannot be compared.

> When you go to the Internet, you type in a word? – I enter 'FRIV'! 'FRIV' – what does that mean? – These are all games … (talk fragment from play-based focus group).

In order to discover the richness of young children's "stories" about digital culture, the idea of a mosaic approach on the various studies as the empirical basis of the chapter is used. The Mosaic approach (Clark & Moss, 2001) originated from early childhood education and was inspired by the "pedagogy of listening", which is based on relations, encounters and dialogues between co-constructers (Rinaldi, 2006, p. 58). Respectively, the construction of children's knowledge and identities is immersed in relations with environment, culture and other human beings. Being open to the other, children and micro-worlds around them, and being sensitive to a great variety of languages children use, pedagogues can hear children's ideas, symbols and codes (Rinaldi, 2006). Listening is an active process of making meaning to what children learn, say, act, construct, and it presents an effort of giving value to the other person. Simultaneously, listening is a process of interpretation and mutual development the listener and the speaker.

Listening to children's perspectives and consulting with them are the basic principles for research *with* children. As the environment for a process of active communication, complex interaction and exchange of meanings between a researcher and a child, it relies on a multitude of young children's languages (Clark, 2005). To listen carefully and to access young children's perspectives on their early experiences, a researcher combines a mosaic of participatory methods, which represent a source for more pieces of the puzzle (Clark, 2005; Clark, McQuail, & Moss, 2003; Clark & Moss, 2001).

In this chapter, I am using the *idea* of this methodological approach, especially the "bringing together [of] different pieces or perspectives in order to create an image of children's worlds, both individual and collective" (Clark, 2005, p. 13). Mosaic, as the creation and unification of the individual elements into wholeness, is certainly related to some methodological issues, including the challenges of triangulation. The possibility of combining different methods, techniques and data, such as images and words (respectively, multifocal children's voices), emphasize the validity, reliability and reflexivity of this approach and idea, especially from the perspective of child-friendliness, authenticity and contextualisation of research with children.

Although mixing and combining data obtained from different methods can be "methodologically risky" (Ilomäki, 2008, p. 50), when used, the multi-method of combining different studies means that each of them can form a piece of a greater whole, which adds new meanings and new insights towards the explored phenomenon (Ilomäki, 2008). For me as a researcher, it is a way to be more creative and to introduce "more human and passionate elements" (Janesick, 2000, p. 394) into the studies I have done.

Finally, viewed as a methodological discussion, the chapter seeks to answer the main question: what are the challenges when shaping a "vivid picture of the everyday life of the child?" (Clark, 2005, p. 13). It assembles pieces of the puzzle gathered from different studies and methods and uses the ideas of the Mosaic approach.

RESEARCH PERSPECTIVES ON CHILDREN AND THEIR DIGITAL WORLD

As in many areas of social life, in the area of growing up in digital context, it is possible to perceive overlapping theories concerning social attention. As the dominant framework of reference, such theories influence the theoretical, empirical, research and common sense questions and answers about the digital practices of young children in the pedagogical community.

The early phase of research on children's computer experiences was formed under the influence of positivism in the social sciences and technical determinism in understanding computer technologies (Pribišev Beleslin, 2011). Among the first studies on children's use of computers were "elegantly designed experiments" (Bronfenbrenner, 1997, p. 30) undertaken within a short time, and decontextualized in terms of space and time in laboratories, *on* children who had not ever seen computers in their everyday environments. The early phase offered reliable data about the influence of new technologies in the area of (cognitive) development of young children, and the body of knowledge was already shaped.

With the increasing availability of computer technology as a form of mass social experiment *in vivo*, the computer culture (Papert, 1980) started to develop, in which children began to live quite passionately. Ideas about children and "children's machines", shifted from being socially- and value-neutral, towards determination as significant "social actors", widely available, and multiple in terms of meanings and values. Such a paradigmatic framework opened up opportunities for new research, orientated to the characteristics, properties and features of digital practices and children's behaviours in interaction with computers. Studies within the much more computerised institutional context of preschool became common, especially with case studies (McPake, Stephen, Plowman, Sime & Downey, 2005) and naturalistic inquiries (Brooker & Siraj-Blatchford, 2002). Once again, this caused the emergence of reliable knowledge about practices related to children's digital experiences.

A new, digital wave is developing under certain socio-technological circumstances: digitalization, the expansion of ethereal internet space which has not yet been fully regulated, the phenomenon of "socialization" of the digital world as well as the mutual transfer of virtual-real features in the (non) spatial community. A frame of reference for researching young children's digital experiences is now given. A new form of children's needs is emerging: the need for virtual social interaction and mutual cyber sharing in often informal online learning communities enables situated and distributed learning (Mayes & Fritas, 2007). On the other hand, the everyday use of digital media by children is not as spectacular, innovative and creative, as was previously expected (Buckingham, 2008). Instead, it is used for entertainment, communication and searching for information (Buckingham, 2008; Pribišev Beleslin, 2012a).

The rise of the digital wave coincides with a paradigm shift that sheds light on "the social construction of childhood" (Prout & James, 1997/2005, p. 20). Research in early childhood, increasingly becomes orientated towards the qualitative paradigmatic dimension (Hatch, 2007), providing a new angle of inquiry that is based on some assumptions. These include: the rights of young children are highly respected within pedagogical contexts (Sommer, Pramling Samuelsson & Hundeide, 2010); the status of young children within an adult-centred society shifted from "becoming human" to "being" (Lee, as cited in Halldén, 2005, p. 5); children are active social agents of their lives and active members of society which they shape as they live in it (Prout and James, 1997/2005); they have hundreds of languages, potentials, competencies (Malaguzzi, see Moss, 1999). The social and cultural contexts are important for considering young children's childhoods, development and learning (Halldén, 2005; Rogoff, 2003).

The active participation of young children in research is based on respecting and accepting their angle of understanding reality as equal as adults (van Berk, 2006; Punch, 2002). Giving children powerful voices in society (Prout & James, 1997/2005) in order to find ways of carefully "listening to young children" (Clark, 2005; Clark & Moss, 2001) in respect of "children's perspectives" (Sommer et al., 2010), opens up the possibilities for inquiring about, the often latent, digital experiences of young children.

THREE STUDIES ON THE DIGITAL EXPERIENCES OF YOUNG CHILDREN IN A LOCAL CONTEXT

I have approached the mosaic as an idea by combining three studies conducted over time as separate entities with different methodological approaches, methods, and languages (Table 1). The underlying reason for putting them together as a natural process lay in the need to experience the results as a meaningful, more comprehensive whole, by listening to the different "voices" from the individual studies on similar phenomena. The origins and evolutionary process of study, "emergent design", was largely determined and defined by the continuity of ideas, as well as experiences during the research, which was also the primary justification for their consideration *post factum* through the lens of a mixed method approach.

At the level of theoretical and research perspectives, I used "paradigmatic mixing legitimation" (Onwuegbuzie & Johnson, 2006, p. 59). This was especially evident in the third study. Previous experiences in data collection and interpretation revealed the need for the new paradigmatic framework. In this way, it was made possible for young children to be "heard" more visibly through the chosen methods and to participate in the co-construction of the body of knowledge about their digital subculture. The limitations of the single paradigmatic framework caused the shift towards a different approach to children as research participants. The right of the children to use their own languages, conceptual meanings and authentic actions was crucial for the research to be participant-friendly, which I aimed for in the third study. Thus, children became equal "informants of their own life worlds" (Christensen & James, 2008, p. 1), and "participate[d] in the design and production of research" (MacNaughton, Smith & Davis, 2007, p 168).

The process of developing research questions had a similar background. These emerged from previous studies (Ilomäki, 2008). The evidence from the first quantitative study opened a field for a research question developed in the second: the need to study children's perception of social practices which largely, but latently, were changing their development. Accordingly, stretching the quantitative research question to encompass the listening to children's stories on everyday practices around ICT steered me towards the paradigmatic perspective of my future researches *with* the children, rather than on or about the children.

As a research design, the Mosaic approach is a way of putting together a lot of pieces of children's lived experiences in a broader picture through dialog, interpretation and reflexion between all research participants (children, parents, practitioners, researchers). Based on the principles which allow researcher to enter into the complex contextualized reality (it is multi-method, participatory, reflexive, adaptable, focussed on children's lived experiences, and embedded into practice), presents a suitable research tool for inquiring the ways children perceive the research phenomena. It has its own stages. First, children and adults together gather the data and research documentation on children's experiences and perspectives within pedagogical institution, and then, in the second stage, a researcher together with participants interpret and reflect on that experiences (Clark & Moss, 2001), constructing the mosaic of knowledge about the phenomenon. For me, in a broader sense, it was a kind of an inspiration and perspective on several different studies with the same research focus, as well as the framework for embedding different results and methodological challenges altogether in a meaningful unity.

Early Computer Experiences and Children's Development

In 2007, I carried out a study on the impact of computer experience on the overall development of young children for my doctoral dissertation (Pribišev Beleslin, 2012). Specific research hypotheses determined the direction of impact and the area of most intense effect. Although the results of the study were unusual, given the previous body of knowledge as well as everyday local discourse, they rendered visible the latent power of early computer experiences.

In the area of the most anticipated negative impacts, physical development, the greatest positive impact occurred, which comprised 13.27% of the total difference. The differences were statistically significant in nine out of ten of the investigated areas of development, for children with advanced computing experience. Furthermore, the study revealed a great homogeneity among children (75.82%) belonging to the group with advanced computing experiences for indicators such as excellence in gross motor skills (running), fine motor skills (handling sports equipment), and the need for physical activity (such as dancing). On the other hand, the physical indicators for children's health, such as obesity, improper posture and poor concentration, did not directly link with computer experience, at least in early childhood. Other words, children use the digital technologies, not as passive recipients, or "victims" of computer technology (Selwyn, 2003), but as active agents of their own lives. Development and digital learning are interrelated processes and are almost holistically changed with the increasing use of computer technology.

However, the study sheds light on some methodological challenges. Simplification of the research results by shattering the one-dimensional variables of complex phenomena, led to simplified conclusions (Hatch, 2007), as well as to a linearity in representing the results. Alienation from oneself as a researcher, which is expressed mostly in the process of writing results "in impersonal, third-person prose" (Denzin & Lincoln, 2000, p. 10), as well as with the source and nature of data acquired second-hand (mediated by questionnaires in the field, as well as statistical procedures in data analysis), constitutes the basic distance from the participants. Researchers can feel that they are completely separated from this stage of data analysis (Janesick, 2000), and return to the figures as refined, foreign and depersonalized data that is entirely valid, reliable and objective. Here, however, the contribution from research methods, as well as statistical analysis and interpretation provides an insight into the possible trends and directions of movement on the part of the phenomenon that I have researched.

Children's Meaning and "Personal Worlds" around Digital Experiences

The second study (Pribisiev Beleslin, 2010) focused on children's drawing where four- and five-year-olds represented themselves using computers. The aim was to highlight children's perspectives on their own computer experiences. Here, I used visual data collected from the same children included in previous study as a source for a separate study. Children's drawings were a mirror for their digital experiences.

Using children's drawings in research with children is a widely accepted method nowadays (Clark & Moss, 2001; Einarsdóttir, 2005, 2007; Punch, 2002; Thomson, 2008), which is sensitive to children's competences (Punch, 2002). Children create drawings within social practice and in the process of a dialogue between a child and the world surrounding him or her. So, it is a kind of children's narration on everyday life (Klerfelt, 2006, Punch, 2002, Thomson, 2008), as well as their living

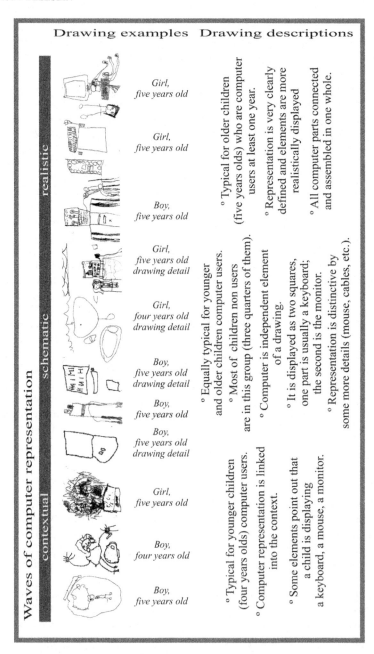

Figure 1. Development of computers representation (Pribišev Beleslin, 2012b, p. 49)

experiences expressed within a non-verbal language (Einarsdóttir, 2007). As a research technique that provides an insight into how a child creates meanings and "personal worlds" using pictorial language, it is a mirror in which the social context is reflected (Klerfelt, 2006).

In the process of analysing, comparing and interpreting the data, and being open-minded towards the data, I dedicated special attention to coding procedures. At the first level of coding, I used an open coding technique, without previously established indicators. The data from the children's drawings initiated the first categories which were descriptive and of low inference (Punch, 1998, p. 206). In a few rounds of open coding, much more generalized and abstract categories, with concept properties, were differentiated. This created the conditions to generalize abstract conceptual categories, higher-order inference pattern codes (Punch, 1998, p. 206), and finally to create "theories", that is, stories about children's computer experiences. Whether it is a central or a secondary theme, a computer or some of its parts, is always recognizable on a child's drawing. The computer representations of non-user children were almost completely the same as the drawings by children with computer experience. Children display computers in their real form, with variations in emphasis on computer parts that are (perhaps) more important to them. The computer was not mystified or defined in the form of somebody/something else (e.g. a surreal human or creature). All children could imagine themselves as self-confident and competent users.

The analysis of the drawings indicated two aspects of children's worlds around computers:
– The development of computer representation has specific stages and common patterns, connected partly with the child's age and drawing ability, but not with computer experiences. Stages are joining in the form of waves and merging one into the other: into contextual, schematic and realistic display, as shown in Figure 1. The uniformity in expression indicates on possible existence of some regularity in visual representation of computer technical properties in young children.
– Children usually and more often present themselves in individualistic activities around computers, and this representation of their experiences has common patterns, which I summarized into three huge categories: "Photographing with computer", "Me and my computer", "I work on the computer". Joint activities of children and others (adults and peers) are notable less commonly, although two larger categories appeared: "Cooperation around computer activities" and "Computer activities are mutual social space" (Figure 2).

Affluence of children's visual expression on the one hand, and a kind of universality within the computer displays, and the activities around, on the other, inspired me to combine the children's visual language and my words. Taken together, as the study results, I have used them to describe the flow and some shared properties of that contextualised development and drawn experiences of children.

Individualistic child – computer activities and relations

"Photographing with computer"

*Girl, five years old
drawing detail*

More girls than boys, mostly older children, look as if they are posing in front of a camera, next to a computer. The children do not intend to show the work process, but to record themselves, their looks, position, emotion, possession of the computer.

"Me and my computer"

Boy, five years old

Children display themselves and the computers in a certain relation, although direct interaction is unrecognizable. Children are not occupied with the display of their activity nor the products of the activities.

The basic theme is the activity of the children; the moment of the action and the very work on the computer. This is shown with the body posture, position of the hands that are always connected with the computer (the child is "typing", clicking or drawing). It displays the process of play and activities (more often with boys) and the products of individual activities (more often with girls).

"I work on the computer"

Boy, five years old

Cooperation around computer activities

"Mutual social space"

Girl, five years old

Adults can be recognized as others, mainly turned toward the child. The process of a mutual activity (singing, conversation) is pleasant for all participants.

"Mutual work on computers"

Children are gathered around the process of an activity "here and now". The other person is very present and involved as an „onlooker" (Freeman & Somerindyke, 2001).

Boy, four years old

Figure 2. Children's activities around computers

As a challenge for the novice researcher in the qualitative paradigm, I was simply overwhelmed by the huge body of data, which was, in some cases, completely different, detailed and hard to understand. Nevertheless, the beauty, richness and meaningfulness of this gave me a power to understand children's perspectives on their computer activities, enclosed in home space. Inner "face-to-face" conversation with authentic data, not transformed into bare numbers, was my "stretching exercise" (Janesick, 2000, p. 386) in the process of refining and continuous reflection upon my understanding of what I could see in the visual data. Furthermore, pictorial language is an environment for adults to hear and understand what is of worth to the child, though "silent" and "unobtrusive" (Hatch, 2002), data gives one dimension of the children's story, and others are still hidden. In research with children, it can be a powerful instrument "to discover a more complete truth than the children are able to tell" (Kyronlampi-Kylmanen & Maatta, 2011, p. 92), and to make new pieces for the puzzle (Clark, 2005).

Although I used authentic visual language to represent the study results, I missed children's words, which could give the titles and lived experiences for categories that had overgrown in the silent world. Instead of giving the names of categories which were actually my words, thoughts, labels, and understandings, in the next study, I tried to include methods of acquiring the data based on children's languages within a play-based situation. Therefore, the triangulation of drawings with other types of data may increase confidence in data analysis (Hatch, 2002, p. 121). This gave it a validation based on contextualization (Onwuegbuzie & Johnson, 2006; Ilomäki, 2008).

Growing up Digitally

In the third study done in 2012, I was interested in how young children's lives are shaped by their every day digital experience, and what are their stories and understandings of social trends with which they are surrounded. "Two research questions reappear: how children experienced digital social lives, and what is important for them in digital culture and practice?" (Pribišev Beleslin, 2014, p. 258). From the children's perspective, I combined participatory methods appropriate to children's competence within a multi-method approach (Clark & Moss, 2001; Punch, 2002; van Berk, 2006). The basic principle used participatory methods in order to listen to everyday children's experiences through an active process of communication, relying on verbal language, but also on different ways children express themselves (play, movement, graphical expressions, emotion, interaction, etc.). For that I used a play-based focus group, combined with task-based techniques, such as drawing and photographing.

A focus group with children under eight years is rarely used, unlike a child-focused interview (Cameron, 2005). One reason could be find in the few characteristics of this research approach: it seeks for views, opinions, thoughts, perspectives of participants and their deeper picture of what is happening (Ryan & Lobman, 2007, see Pribišev Beleslin, 2014). So, maturity of participants is expected to some degree. In addition, it mimics social practice, so focus groups with five- and six-year-olds, should rely on situational speech and play, through allowing children to use "kinetic language" (Docherty & Sandelowski, 1999). In my study, as a researcher I used a doll to facilitate focus groups to provide non-literality (Johnson, Christie, & Yawkey, 1999), one of the key dimensions of play in research with young children. Using the doll provided immediate and eased contact, even without much introduction, and shifted the outer frame around the child in the inner reality that is an "'As-if' stance toward reality" (Johnson et al., p. 16). Within it, the children focused on the "researcher" and entered into a conversation, listened to each other, and answered the questions posted by the "researcher doll". The doll was an "architect" (Clark, 2005) that created a research environment close to everyday experiences so it was meaningful, relaxing and enjoyable for the children. The doll undertook contextualised conversation focusing them on research questions (Ryan & Lobman, 2007), within which the children were directed to their preferences (Harden, Scott, Backett-Milburn, & Jackson, 2000). Play-like research areas give children the opportunity to have control over their story, to add their story elements, and to form the characteristics of group dynamics.

Given the diversity of the data (visual and verbal), I used the inductive method of analysis, flexible and suitable for multiple qualitative paradigms (Hatch, 2002). During the first reading of the data, I redisplayed data within the categories based on the main issues in the focus group and with some assumptions from previous studies. After several re-readings and open coding, and creating several domains based on semantic and visual relationships, frames of analysis (Hatch, 2002, p. 162) were constructed, showing the priorities and meanings that young children constructed living immersed in new technologies. For them, a digital environment is a natural, amicable milieu, integrated into their everyday lives, especially their home environment. Interconnected with play, leisure time, friendship and a sense of belonging to family, the everyday usage of digital technologies is not so creative, innovative and spectacular as it is coveted within an adult perspective (Buckingham, 2008).

> … What children like to do on the computer? – To play … – I like to watch cartoon Pepa Pig … – I like it, too … I love to play computer games, to draw the stories – I prefer to listen to the story Shir Khan. – What else? What do you think children like to do on the computer? – I play games – I like to play games …. (Talk fragment from play-based focus group)

Computer time, in which it is impossible to discern the actual time that one is on the Internet, is equally significant as a source for learning as it is for entertainment. For children, the areas of benefits are: learning how to play computer games, developing academic achievement in order to be successful in school, establishing competences for "adulthood", watching cartoons in free time, as well as improving the technical competences.

> What do you think children can learn while playing on computers? – Learn to draw … – Learn to play games … – I can learn numbers … – Learn letters …

> … To play computer games to grow up and then I can go into the depth of the sea ….

… So when they grow up big when they go to school when a teacher asks them to tell what they have learned … – So, when the children use the computer they learn letters and numbers? – And then the teacher may ask and then they get a five when say something …. (Talk fragments from the play-based focus groups)

For children, the Internet appears to be an available space, yet abstruse, but they are confidently developing the skills for coping with it. It is useful for "tapping" keys and finding "everything you want", but also, for having fun and communicating with others, especially with relatives via mail and on social networks.

… What can children learn while playing on the computer? – Well, games. – When I typed "ve-ve dot com", it is not something, there is no games. There's something stupid, I go on and find the one with that black and … – I find a game 'free' there are some Black Man …. (Talk fragment from the play-based focus group)

Distinct are stories on cultures of communities immersed in digital practise. Digital culture of peer community is built in the mutual children's interaction around computers through activities such as the computer games or watching cartoons. More often children talk about communities of brothers and sisters, where are established different relations. Older children help the younger ones for running programs, helping through levels in games, finding information on the Internet or typing in keywords. Sometimes, siblings are arguing about the order of usage, setting rules and games around digital technologies. But, children rarely talk about peers and their friends they meet at home ("I play games with my friend in pairs", comment on drawing).

Relations of adults and children in the digital culture, is usually on the beginning of the game, when a child needs help in entering a computer game, or finding games on the Internet ("My dad turned on", comment on drawing). However, the children and parent play together ("It's me and father, he taught me to play the game, he plays a formula, and I Ben Ten", comment on drawing). Adults set the rules and discipline.

Children's everyday stories on daily rituals of family presents a frequent topic of children's drawings: descriptions of the moment of the daily life of the family, with relaxed atmosphere where children use computers, such as afternoon leisure, cooking dinner, parents playing with young children and so on. On the other hand, loneliness and fear of the dark appears in almost all focus groups:

… So, until we go to sleep …

… Often feel lonely … and I am in darkness … And I am not afraid of anything … – But, I am afraid. (Talk fragments from the play-based focus groups)

In the methodological sense, "allowing" that research area has become contextualized by childhood (Pribišev Beleslin, 2014) and "situated activity that

109

locates the observer in the world" as Denzin and Lincoln (2000, p. 3) mentioned (per techniques that are close to young children's ways of learning, through making relations, doing and playing) balances the power position in the hierarchy of adults and children in research. Task-based methods (Punch, 2002), as well as participatory techniques (drawing, photography, making maps, records, itineraries and, web charts with children, etc.) and other structured and multi-sensory methods such as role play activities, participatory games and the use of puppets (Clark et al., 2003) allow careful listening and multidimensional understanding about the digital experiences of four- five- and six-year-old children.

At the level of personality and the ethics of researchers and research participants within a participatory approach, the issue of self-reflection emerged. One aspect of this is the development of a multitude of relationships with the children in play-based focus groups, which demanded self-reflection during the dialogue with the children, as well as continuously staying within the role as a "doll researcher". This leads to the loss of researcher identity (Pribišev Beleslin, 2014), insofar as the children are paying attention to a doll researcher and not me. On the other hand, external modes of respecting ethical issues (Table 1) have increased through the studies' flow. In the process of gathering and interpreting qualitative data, I encountered personal, real and contextual data, around which I was able to imagine the real events that marked them and to which I could return many times. In relation to the quantitative data from the first study and the one-dimensional data from the second, within this third study there was an interplay between me as a researcher and the children's participation in its design and construction. I provided a methods framework and focused their thinking on the process of data collection. Through the methods of data narrowing towards the generation of more abstract categories in the process of analysis and interpretation, I was in a continual "face-to-face" dialogue with the data, mirroring the studied context.

FUTURE ISSUES – WHAT IS MISSING?

In the sense of meta-position for different studies of the same phenomena, the idea of mosaic can be helpful, but it can be also used as an inspiration for constructing a more comprehensive and detailed understanding of the lived experiences of children growing up digitally in the changing world. Indeed, many pieces from different dimensions in which children are living their digital childhood can be reached by different ways and further cycles of inquiries. Many are missing. In particular, the piece that illustrates the practice of children in their natural environment – home – is missing, where they are often "alone up to the dark" (talk fragment from play-based focus group with five-year-olds) when it comes to using new technologies spontaneously. Other lacking parts include what parents would say – their perspectives on children's digital experience. For instance, what are their beliefs, and do they celebrate children's competence, or are they a little afraid of their digital experiences? Of particular concern is the lack of parts that illustrate the institutional scaffolding, where the mosaic has remained unfinished for more than a decade. Does the unconscious educational environment as the "last analogue oasis" affect the social digital divide, bearing in mind that children by themselves go beyond the technical one? That is a question for further cycles of inquiry.

In a methodological sense, we can approach a new cycle of discovering these disguised places of young children. One idea and method is to adopt the Mosaic approach as one of the possible languages to reach children's tacit perspectives, voices and contexts.

REFERENCES

Bronfenbrenner, U. (1997). *Ecology of human development.* Beograd: Institute for Publishing Textbooks.

Brooker, L., & Siraj-Blatchford, J. (2002). "Click on the miaow!": How children of 3 and 4 experience the nursery computer. *Contemporary Issues in Early Childhood, 3*(2), 251-273.

Buckingham, D. (2008). Introducing identity. In D. Buckingham (Ed.), *Youth, identity, and digital media* (pp. 1-24). Cambridge, MA: The MIT Press.

Cameron, H. (2005). Asking the tough questions: A guide to ethical practices in interviewing young children. *Early Child Development and Care, 175*(5), 597-610.

Christensen, P. M., & James, A. (2008). Introduction: Researching children and the childhood culture of communication. In P. M. Christensen & A. James (Eds.), *Researching with children. Perspectives and practices* (2nd edition, pp. 1-9). New York, NY: Routledge Taylor & Francis Group.

Clark, A., & Moss, P. (2001). *Listening to young children: The Mosaic approach.* London: National Children's Bureau for the Joseph Rowntree Foundation.

Clark, A., McQuail, S., & Moss, P. (2003). *Exploring the field of listening to and consulting with young children* (Research Report RR445). London: Department for Education and Skills.

Clark, A. (2005). Ways of seeing: Using the Mosaic approach to listen to young children's perspectives. In A. Clark, A. T. Kjørholt, & P. Moss (Eds.), *Beyond listening. Children's perspectives on early childhood services* (pp. 29-49). Bristol: Policy Press.

Denzin, N. K., & Lincoln, Y. S. (2000). Introduction: The discipline and practice of qualitative research. In N. K. Denzin & Y. S. Lincoln (Eds.), *Handbook of qualitative research* (2nd edition, pp. 1-29). Thousand Oaks/London/New Delhi: Sage.

Docherty, S., & Sandelowski, M. (1999). Focus on qualitative methods: Interviewing children. *Research in Nursing & Health, 22,* 177-185.

Einarsdóttir, J. (2005). Playschool in pictures: Children's photographs as a research method. *Early Child Development and Care, 175*(6), 523-541.

Einarsdóttir, J. (2007). Research with children: Methodological and ethical challenges. *European Early Childhood Education Research Journal, 15*(2), 197-211.

Freeman, N. K., & Somerindyke, J. (2001). Social play at the computer: Preschoolers scaffold and support peers' computer competence. *Information Technology in Childhood Education Annual, 1,* 203-213.

Halldén, G. (2005, November). *The metaphors of childhood in a preschool context.* A paper presented at the AARE conference, Sydney, Australia. Retrieved from www.aare.edu.au/05pap/hal05001.pdf.

Harden, J., Scott, S., Backett-Milburn, K., & Jackson, S. (2000). Can't talk, won't talk? Methodological issues in researching children. *Sociological Research Online, 5*(2).

Hatch, A. J. (2002). *Doing qualitative research in education settings.* Albany, NY: State University of New York Press.

Hatch, A. J. (Ed.). (2007). *Early childhood qualitative research.* New York, NY: Routledge.

Ilomaki, L. (2008). *The effects of ICT on school: Teachers' and students' perspectives.* Doctoral Dissertation. Department of Teacher Education, University of Turku, Painosalama Oy, Turku, Finland. Retrieved from https://www.doria.fi/bitstream/handle/10024/42311/B314.pdf?sequence=3

Janesick, V. J. (2000). The choreography of qualitative research design: Minuets, improvisations, and crystallization. In N. K. Denzin & Y. S. Lincoln (Eds.), *Handbook of qualitative research* (2nd edition, pp. 379-400). Thousand Oaks/London/New Delhi: Sage.

Johnson, J. E., Christie, J. F., & Yawkey, T. D. (1999). *Play and early childhood development* (2nd edition). New York, NY: Addison Wesley Longman, Inc.

Klerfelt, A. (2006). Cyberage Narratives: Creative computing in after-school centres. *Childhood, 13*(2), 175-203.

Kyronlampi-Kylmanen, T., & Maatta, K. (2011). Using children as research subjects: How to interview a child aged 5 to 7 years. *Educational Research and Reviews, 6*(1), 87-93.

MacNaughton, G., Smith, K., & Davis, K. (2007). Researching with children: The challenges and possibilities for building "child friendly" research. In J. A. Hatch (Ed.), *Early childhood qualitative research* (pp. 167-184). New York, NY: Routledge.

Mayes, T., & de Fritas, S. (2007). Learning and e-learning, In H. Beetham & R. Sharpe (Eds.), *Rethinking pedagogy for a digital era. Designing and delivering e-learning* (pp. 13-25). London/New York, NY: Routledge.

McPake, J., Stephen, C, Plowman, L., Sime, D., & Downey, S. (2005). *Already at a disadvantage? ICT in the home and children's preparation for primary school.* University of Stirling and Becta, ICT Research Bursaries. Retrieved from The University of York website: http://www.york.ac.uk/res/e-society/projects/3/already_disadvantage.pdf.

Moss, P. (1999). Early childhood institutions as a democratic and emancipatory project. In L. Abbott, & H. Moylett (Eds.), *Early education transformed* (pp. 142-153). New York, NY: Taylor & Francis e-Library.

Onwuegbuzie, A. J., & Johnson, R. B. (2006). The validity issue in mixed research. *Research in the Schools, 13*(1), 48-63.

Papert, S. (1980). *Mindstorms: Children, computers and powerful ideas.* New York, NY: Basic Books.

Pribišev Beleslin, T. (2010, August). *What we can "hear" when we "listen" to children's drawings about their computer experiences.* Paper presented at OMEP XXVI World Congress "Children. Citizens in a challenged world". Göteborg, Sweden.

Pribišev Beleslin, T. (2011). *Children's computer experiences: Implications for early childhood education.* Banja Luka: Filozofski fakultet.

Pribišev Beleslin, T. (2012). Digital growing-up of students and education in the post information era. In T. Duronjić (Ed.), *Internet culture of students in The Republic of Srpska* (pp. 47-61). Banja Luka: Faculty of Political Sciences.

Pribišev Beleslin, T. (2012b). Early childhood education and up-bringing in postinformational era: A look at the growing up digitally and digital divide of young children. In I. Pehlić, E. Vejo, & A. Hasanagić (Eds.), *Contemporary trends in early education. Scientific monography* (pp. 39-56). Banja Luka: Faculty of Islamic Education of the University of Zenica.

Pribišev Beleslin, T. (2014). Play in research with children. *Croatian Journal of Education, 16,* Sp.Ed.No. 1/2014, 253-266.

Prout, A., & James, A. (1997/2005). A new paradigm for the sociology of childhood? Provenance, promise and problems. In A. James & A. Prout (Eds.), *Constructing and reconstructing childhood: Contemporary issues in the sociological study of childhood* (pp. 7-32). London/Washington, DC: Taylor & Francis e-Library.

Punch. K. F. (1998). *Introduction to social research: Quantitative and qualitative approaches.* London/Thousand Oaks/New Delhi: SAGE Publications.

Punch, S. (2002). Research with children. The same or different from research with adults? *Childhood, 9*(3), 321-341.

Rinaldi, C. (2006). *In dialog with Reggio Emilia. Listening, researching and learning.* London/New York, NY: Routledge.

Rogoff, B. (2003). *The cultural nature of human development.* New York, NY: Oxford University Press.

Ryan, S., & Lobman, C. (2007). The potential of focus groups to inform early childhood policy and practice. In A. J. Hatch (Ed.), *Early childhood qualitative research* (pp. 63-74). New York, NY: Routledge.

Selwyn, N. (2003). 'Doing IT for the kids': Re-examining children, computers and the 'information society'. *Media, Culture & Society, 25*, 351-378.

Sommer, D., Pramling Samuelsson, I., & Hundeide, K. (2010). *Child perspectives and children's perspectives in theory and practice.* London/New York, NY: Springer.

Thomson, P. (2008). Children and young people's voices in visual research. In P. Thomson (Ed.), *Doing visual research with children and young people* (pp. 1-20). New York, NY: Routledge.

van Berk, L. (2006). Working with children in development. In V. Desai & R. Potter (Eds.), *Doing development research* (pp. 52-61). London/Thousand Oaks/ New Delhi: Sage.

Tamara Pribišev Beleslin
Faculty of Philosophy
University of Banja Luka
Republic of Srpska

JACOB DAVIDSEN AND RUBEN VANDERLINDE

8. EXPLORING WHAT TOUCH-SCREENS OFFER FROM THE PERSPECTIVES OF CHILDREN

Methodological Challenges

INTRODUCTION

How can we study children's interaction in a technology-rich environment from the perspectives of children? How can children's perspectives shine a light on the teacher's designs for activities and materials in a technology-rich environment? One approach to address these questions could be using questionnaires or survey data. For example, we could send out questionnaires to school management or teachers asking about children's use of information and communication technologies (ICT) in schools and classrooms. Potential questions could include: Do children have access to ICT in classrooms? Is ICT a tool that supports children in their learning activities? We would probably receive a sufficient number of responses to make generalisations about the level of children's use of ICT in an individual school or classroom. These results could be compared across schools on various parameters, such as the number of computers in classrooms, children's access to computers and types of activities carried out using computers. We might conclude that teachers need further training to better integrate ICT in their pedagogical thinking and activities, and that every child should have access to ICT on a daily basis. Nevertheless, this kind of research approach cannot describe and represent how children actually use ICT in learning activities or how teachers guide children. More precisely, questionnaires provide information on the more general level, whereas a micro multimodal perspective focuses on the nano curriculum level (Akker, Kuiper, & Hameyer, 2003), referring to the level of the individual learner. This means an analysis on how children actually learn and collaborate supported by ICT. To put differently, by studying the nano curriculum level in a micro multimodal perspective, we orient our analysis towards how pairs of children collaborate through language, gestures and the material.

Selwyn, Potter and Cranmer (2010) argued that taking children's views could play an important role in informing the future use of ICT in classrooms. They suggested that focusing on children's perspectives could shed light on how children actually use ICT, and further, that this perspective could inform a bottom-up technology innovation and integration process. By using questionnaires, interviews and drawing activities with children, Selwyn et al. (2010) provided a rich understanding of children's perspectives on ICT in the context of British primary schools. Nevertheless, the research design applied by Selwyn et al. (2010)

G.B. Gudmundsdottir and K.B. Vasbø (Eds.), Methodological Challenges When Exploring Digital Learning Spaces in Education, 115–132.

distanced itself from studying what children actually do with ICT in learning activities. To put differently, there is a difference between analysing what children *say they do* and analysing how their learning activities with ICT actually unfolds. Consequently, we argue that researchers need to get closer to the phenomenon in question: children's everyday interaction with ICT in classroom environments. The methodological orientation towards studying children's actions in practice is grounded in the work of Goodwin (2000), Koschmann and LeBaron (2002), and Streeck, Goodwin and LeBaron (2011). Findings from such studies illustrate the power of studying how participants make sense in the situation by using language, gestures and the material at hand. From a curriculum perspective, this is called the nano level (Akker, Kuiper, & Hameyer, 2003), pointing at the level of the individual learner. Overall, ICT researchers are challenged to shift their perspective from the system, school and teacher level to a detailed interactional level taking children's natural activities, interactions and experiences into account. This situated and micro-analytic perspective on children's use of ICT in classroom settings contrasts with the perspective of the questionnaires usually sent to school management and teachers.

On this basis, we make a plea for researchers to study how children actually construct meaningful trajectories with ICT in collaborative learning activities. By applying a micro multimodal perspective, a more in-depth and situated understanding of children's use of ICT in practice is offered. Hence, we present a research design for exploring educational ICT use at the nano curriculum level and from the perspectives of the children. This design is based on methodological traditions such as conversation analysis (Goodwin, 2000; Streeck, Goodwin, & LeBaron, 2011) and interaction analysis (Jordan & Henderson, 1995), and relates to ethnomethodology (Heritage, 1984). The underlying assumption across these different methodological perspectives is that human interaction is situated, and that participants show their understanding of each other's actions through their continued orientation to the shared construction of meaning through language, gestures and the use of materials. Ivarsson (2003), Klerfelt (2007), Koschmann and LeBaron (2002), Roth (2001), and Ryberg (2007) – to name some researchers applying a similar design – have shown the power of doing micro analytic studies of interaction. For instance, Klerfelt (2007) showed the importance of studying and understanding children's gestures while using computers by presenting and analysing small excerpts of interaction. Similarly, Roth (2001) claimed that gestures reveal children's understanding of a concept prior to verbal articulation. In other words, previous micro analytic studies of children have taught us to pay attention to their gestures, body, language and the materials at hand.

Consequently, the concept of the children's perspectives in this chapter focuses on how the children actually collaborate with ICT, materialised as touch-screens in this case. Whereas Selwyn, Potter and Cranmer (2010) focussed on children's interpretation of the use of ICT, we study what they actually do (Blomberg, Giacomi, Mosher, & Swenton-Wall, 1993; Goodwin, 2000; Heritage, 1984) with ICT. Essentially, a distinction can be made between what people say they do and what they actually do (Blomberg et al., 1993). As Christensen and James (2008) suggested, researchers need to change their approach from conducting research *on* children to researching *with* children – thereby promoting the voice of children. Overall, this type of analysis is rather unusual in ICT integration research and curriculum studies, where the majority of studies have focussed on schools and teachers (Vanderlinde, 2011) and thus ignored the children.

The overall theme of this book is to highlight and discuss the methodological challenges faced when exploring digital learning spaces in education. This chapter presents specific challenges from a single case-study school that has integrated touch-screens. The digital learning space in this case is the technology-rich environment with touch-screens at the school. In this environment, researchers and teachers explored how pairs of children interacted with touch-screens in peer-to-peer learning activities. Furthermore, the study explored if mutual engagement and co-learning between teachers and researchers could inform both researchers' and teachers' understanding of children's actual use of ICT.

FOCUS OF THIS STUDY

Recently, a number of publications (e.g. Luckin et al., 2012; Selwyn, 2011) suggested studying the use of ICT in classrooms in more integrative ways. This approach is combinatory by nature, and utilises a variety of research perspectives in the analysis of a given phenomenon. This is in contrast to a pure technical evaluation or a heuristic evaluation of the learning material. Hence, the overall argument is that this form of integrative research approach can provide a more holistic understanding of the use and needs of ICT in schools.

Luckin et al. (2012) referred to a gap between the researcher's knowledge and the practitioner's operationalisation of this knowledge in practice. For example, they stated that "good ideas developed in academic research are not yet filtering through to the classroom" (Luckin et al., 2012, p. 19). In a similar fashion, Selwyn (2011) argued that a change of vocabulary is required to avoid a technical-oriented debate about the future of education, and proposed that learners, teachers and others involved in the daily life of education should be given a voice in the debate about the future of educational technology. Consequently, research should empower the learners and teachers in the discussion and decision-making process regarding ICT in schools. In other words, understanding technology in itself is simply not sufficient; we need to understand technology in use. This demands a nano perspective on curriculum development that takes the voices of children and teachers into account. Hence, the purpose of this chapter is to present and discuss two intertwined methodological challenges to conducting research at the nano curriculum level in ICT integration studies:
– Challenge one: How can researchers obtain children's perspectives on ICT integration research?
– Challenge two: How can researchers inform teacher's designs for activities and materials relating to children's collaboration with ICT?
First, we present a research design with the intention of describing how researchers and teachers can get closer to an understanding of children's actions in peer-to-peer

learning activities in a touch-screen environment. To illustrate this we provide a micro multimodal analysis (Norris, 2004; Streeck et al., 2011) of two children working together in front of a touch-screen. This kind of analysis is in contrast to recent findings from experimental and design related studies of children's collaboration with interactive touch-screens (see for instance Davidsen & Christiansen, 2013). In our analysis, we present what actually happens between the two children using pictures and transcripts of language and gestures. This analysis extends to the second methodological challenge: how best to describe and present children's collaborative action to facilitate dialogue and reflection among teachers and inform their process of designing activities and materials for the touch-screens. In other words, we show that video excerpts and multimodal transcripts can provide teachers with "boundary objects" (Derry et al., 2010; Star, 1989), referring to objects that can facilitate dialogue and knowledge building about one's own practice. Experiences from this research project show that the use of video data and multimodal renderings can bring researchers and teachers closer to a mutual understanding of how children's activities in a touch-screen environment actually unfold. Consequently, this research design can inform teachers' designs for materials and activities.

We should clarify a few concepts before presenting the touch-screen environment. Inspired by Suthers' (2006) notion of an intersubjective epistemology and Stahl's (2006) theoretical orientation of group cognition, we refer to children's situated sense-making when using the term "collaboration" (Davidsen & Christiansen, 2013). Following this, the level of collaboration cannot be decoded by comparing specific types of speech acts, or by looking at the number of utterances or gestures produced by the individual child in peer work. Stahl (2006) referred to this as a coding and counting approach, and concluded that such an approach overlooked the essential characteristics of collaborative learning. Hence, the analysis of the children's collaboration and use of the touch-screens in this research project is oriented towards the children's situated negotiation of meaning in language, gestures and materials. Crook (1994) provided a similar argument, and stated that although effective collaboration among young children is strikingly rare, computers and the concept of collaboration holds an intriguing, yet unexplored, potential for learning. Additionally, Crook argued for viewing the computer as a resource for collaboration, not just a technical fix. Recently, Luckin et al. (2012) concluded that collaboration, or what they term "learning with others", is integrated less frequently into classrooms because it is an unclear concept for teachers.

Furthermore, we should comment on the concept of "children's perspectives". As noted by Selwyn, Potter and Cranmer (2010), children's perspectives is often neglected in the discussion about the past, present and future use and integration of educational ICT. However, taking the perspectives of children is not simply a matter of asking them questions about their use of ICT in and out of schools. Interviews, questionnaires and experiments provide useful insights, but as Blomberg et al. (1993) argued, children (users in general) often know more than they can articulate, which is referred to as a say/do problem of ethnographic work.

Orr (1996) stressed and extended this point by, claiming that "Of course, those of whom the ethnographer is trying to make sense may be in the act of making sense of their situation for themselves" (1996, p. 13). Hence, it is an illusion that interviews and surveys alone can contribute to an understanding of the complexities of a practice from the participant's perspectives. Consequently, we argue that video analysis provides a profound opportunity to study and present children's perspectives of technology-rich environments.

In summary, the focus of this chapter is to present the methodological underpinnings of the children's perspectives, and illustrate and discuss how teachers can design activities and materials based on this perspective.

A PEEK INTO THE TOUCH-SCREEN ENVIRONMENT

The methodological challenges explored in this chapter arise from a broader PhD project at a Danish primary school.[i] Throughout a year-long project (2009–2010) called "Move and Learn" (Davidsen & Georgsen, 2010), children, teachers and researchers explored the affordances of touch-screens in collaborative learning activities. In two classrooms, eight 23-inch interactive touch-screens were integrated into the daily activities of children aged eight and nine. Moreover, one interactive whiteboard (IWB) was provided for teachers and children in both classrooms (Davidsen & Georgsen, 2010).

In total, forty-one children and three teachers participated in the research project. These teachers (Anne, Ben and Claire) did not have any prior experience with the touch-screen technology, but had used traditional computers in their teaching for a couple of years. An illustration of the physical arrangement of the touch-screen environment is provided below:

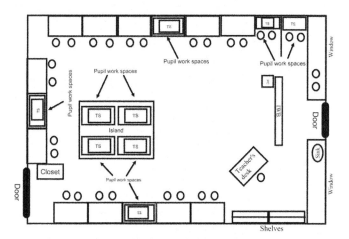

Figure 1. Touch-screen (TS) environment

As stated, the touch-screens were introduced into the classroom environment as a tool for the children to use in various learning activities. Hence, ICT was not a subject on its own (e.g. learning to handle the computer), but was integrated across subjects in a variety of activities and learning materials. In other words, the children were not just learning to use the computers in dedicated labs, but they learned to use the computers in relation to specific subjects in their classrooms. In this innovative "learning space", the children were encouraged to collaborate, negotiate and communicate in pairs while working with the touch-screens. Moreover, the teachers took a position as a guide or a coach (Davidsen & Georgsen, 2010) to scaffold children's collaboration, interaction and dialogue.

OVERALL RESEARCH DESIGN

This particular research project sought to establish a "co-learning agreement" (Wagner, 1997) between the teachers and the researchers guided by the principal of mutual learning through dialogue (Nielsen, Dirckinck-Holmfeld, & Danielsen, 2003). To establish such a relationship, the researchers participated in the daily classroom activities, interviewed the children and the teachers, photographed a variety of situations and collected the digital learning materials designed by the teachers. In addition, the teachers reflected on the project on a collective blog. Most importantly, the data collection encompassed more than 150 hours of video footage captured from seven different positions in the two classrooms. We positioned the cameras above the children to capture their interaction with each other and the touch-screens in their peer-to-peer learning activities.

Figure 2. Camera setup

On a daily basis, the teachers turned on the cameras when the children were working with the single touch-screens. This video data represents the nano curriculum level – the individual learner in practice – and is the primary data source enabling researchers to analyse the children's interaction. Furthermore, the video data was used to facilitate dialogue and learning between researchers and teachers during video feedback sessions, in which the researchers showed the teachers selected video footage and provided transcripts (Davidsen & Vanderlinde, 2014). Together, the researchers and teachers discussed what happened between the children to better understand and redesign the learning materials and activities.

In brief, the study described in this chapter is characterised by its iterative design and its engagement of the practitioners in the research process (see McKenney & Reeves, 2012), with an emphasis on the children's perspectives of peer-to-peer learning activities with touch-screens. Hence, this is not an evaluative study on the effect of touch-screens on learning outcomes; rather it provides a perspective on what played out in the children's everyday activities in the touch-screen environment. We used the video data to provide illustrative multimodal renderings of children's collaboration with the touch-screen as a mediating tool.

A FRAGMENT OF INTERACTION FROM A TOUCH-SCREEN ENVIRONMENT

We present and analyse a short video fragment to demonstrate how the children collaborated while supported by the touch-screens. In total, we provide and analyse 22 seconds of footage with a multimodal transcript to serve a twofold purpose. The first is to show how the children interacted and collaborated in front of the touch-screen, and the second is to show how a multimodal rendering can provide the children's perspectives. This fragment serves as a powerful illustration of how the children collaborated, supported by the touch-screen, and further it provides a background for presenting the two methodological challenges explored in the next section. This brief analysis shows how embodied meaning-making plays out between Iris and Vince, both nine years old and working on a shared touch-screen with the teacher's material (Davidsen & Christiansen, 2013).

Figure 3. Iris and Vince in front of the touch-screen

In this situation, the two children displayed, produced and maintained a mutual understanding of the activity using language, gestures and the manipulation of objects on the touch-screen. This specific situation formed part of an overall activity about the Christian religious tradition of Easter. Initially, the whole class talked about what characterises this religious tradition before, in pairs, the children read about Good Friday, tested their knowledge in a multiple choice quiz and rewrote the story in their own words. To show what they have learned, the children had to make a video using the collaborative software (e.g. Smart Notebook™) on the touch-screen. The children wore headsets with microphones to record and listen to their video. The teacher had instructed the children in video production, e.g. how to use the video screen recorder and how to construct a multimodal story. In this selected fragment, the children should produce a video story using the figures on the screen:

Figure 4. Scenery and figures for the video story

The children were actually rehearsing their video production in this fragment. Beforehand, the children had written their retelling of the story of Good Friday in the booklet in Vince's right hand. The children should then produce a video story with the figures and scenery (Figure 4) provided by the teacher. Vince and Iris, initially began to discuss who should read the text and who should move the figures. After a short discussion, they decided to divide the work between them and agreed to change after the first trial so that both of them got to try moving around the objects and reading the story aloud. Figure 5 provides the fragment of 22 seconds as a series of still photos including transcribed talk in speech bubbles and movement described above the photos. Each frame is numbered and three frames are equal to one second of time[ii]:

Iris moves her left hand towards the booklet and turns her head to the right looking at the booklet in Vince' hand (frame 1-5)

Iris retracts her left hand to her mouth and turns her head right looking directly at Vince (frame 6-10)

Iris keeps her left hand close to her mouth and the right hand on the table, while she slowly turns her head left looking directly at the screen (frame 12-15)

Iris stretches out her left arm towards the screen (19-20)

Iris touches the screen with her left index finger and moves Jesus to the left (frame 21-24)
Vince places the booklet on the table with his right hand (frame 21-23)

Iris turns her head, gazes towards Vince with her left elbow on the table (frame 26-30)
Vince moves his left hand towards his upper torso grabing the headset line, then he snaps twice with his left hand (frame 28-29) Iris strethes out her index finger on her left hand (frame 30)

Iris holds that position (frame 30-35) while Vince positions his left hand on the table (frame 31-34)

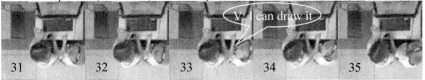

Iris leans slowly forward towards the screen - the body follows her finger – and moves the scrollbar up and as a consequence the figure of Jesus disappears from the screen (frame 36-39)
Vince lifts both his hands up to his head and lifts the headset from his ears twice, but ends up letting it sit on his head (frame 36-40)

Iris removes her finger from the screen and turns her palm up as she retracts her hand from the screeen (frame 41-44)

Vince moves his left hand towards the screen (frame 43-45)

and selects the free hand drawing tool - fingers are spread and right hand is placed on the table (frame 46-50)
Iris moves her left hand towards the screen slowly (frame 47-53)

Vince retracts his hand a liltle from the screen and moves it left - points the palm tree (frame 51-55) - see *Figure 4*
Iris is keeping her hand close to the screen and very close to Vince's left hand (frame 52-61)

Vince moves his finger in a circular movement drawing his version of the rock (frame 56-60)

Vince retracts his hand from the screen and holds it just above the table (frame 61-63)

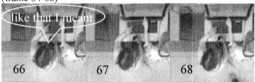

Vince moves his hand toward the screen and extends his index finger out - in the middle of the screen (frame 64-68)

Figure 5. Multimodal rendering of the children's interactions

Without going into a complete analysis, we present a short overview of this multimodal rendering that serves as an illustration and definition of the children's perspectives.

In frame 4-5, Vince turned the booklet around and Iris said, "well that's it". This comment marked the end of their rehearsal. One-and-a-half seconds later, Iris and Vince turned their heads towards each other (frame 11-12). Then, in frame 12-14 Vince asked, "didn't it sound fine?". By using "didn't", Vince showed some uncertainty about his own reading. To put it differently, Vince was asking Iris to evaluate his reading, or he acknowledged some kind of problem and now wanted to know more about it. Iris turned her head around facing the screen before answering Vince (frame 12-16). This movement towards the screen amplified her interest in something else than Vince' reading aloud. In other words, Iris stressed her interest in the missing object through language, but certainly also through her bodily orientation towards the screen. This body movement also served as a way of expressing that Iris at this point in time had no interest in Vince' reading. Iris first started speaking when Vince was looking at the screen. Then, Iris commented on Vince's reading with two words "YEAH but" (frame 16-17). These two words, worked as a way of changing the direction of the activity. Iris was not completely satisfied with his reading, but there were more important things to consider first.

Later, (frame 17-25) Iris elaborated on this matter, saying "it's because we don't have a cave we can put him in-a stone-can we put in front", and moved the figure of Jesus around on the screen while she was talking. By combining talk and movement, Iris was building a multimodal argument. By using Goodwin's (2000) terminology, Iris was making use of different semiotic resources to build a stronger argument. Furthermore, it became easier for Vince to understand her concerns and provide the necessary feedback. Vince replied with a gesture in frame 28-29, snapping with his left hand twice. Afterwards, Vince turned his head to the left looking directly at Iris and said, "I can draw it (.) NO WE CAN DRAW IT of course" in frames 33-34 and 36-38. Interestingly, Vince selected himself at first; however, he changed his allocation of agency and coordination of contributions to the dyad by then using "we". This illustrated an understanding of how the two children had agreed to work together. It was not a spoken rule, but something inherently embedded in their collaborative work. In the final part of his turn, Vince said "of course". This can be understood on two levels; as a correction of himself and as way of saying "no problem, we can easily draw this rock together".

In the next part of the situation, Vince sat with his hands on top of his head while Iris moved her left hand towards the screen, and finally she moved the scrollbar up. Afterwards, Iris retracted her hand from the screen and turned her hand around; her palm faced up and she said "yes of course, we can (0.3) but ehmm he is in the field below" (frame 42-47). This was a confirmation of Vince's suggestion to draw a rock and Vince accepted what looked like a gestural invitation from Iris prior to her verbal turn. Vince performed the action of drawing a rock to cover Jesus with the freehand drawing tool. In the same second, Iris showed her disagreement with the way Vince drew the rock; first saying "NO NOT LIKE THAT" and then "no we don't draw it like that" (frame 49-50 and 53-55). Interestingly, Vince continued drawing the rock for a few seconds, actually finishing his freehand drawing. Vince asked for a clarification from Iris, saying "then how?" (frame 59-60). Iris replied "it is not what I meant: (.) it's not exactly like that I meant" immediately after she agreed on the drawing of the rock. At this point in time Iris was not approving Vince' drawing, but on the other hand she could not articulate what she actually wanted. While Vince drew his version of the rock, Iris showed her disagreement in language. Additionally, she stretched out her left arm towards the screen. Interestingly, she only kept her hand close to the screen and Vince's arm (frame 49-61) without interrupting what Vince was doing. It seemed Iris reserved the next turn at the touch-screen without interrupting Vince's movement physically.

In contrast to the majority of studies of children's collaboration with interactive tabletops and touch-screens which emphasis equality in terms of verbal and physical participation (see Davidsen and Christiansen, 2013, for a review), the study presented in this chapter differs. Not only because of its emphasis on the nano curriculum level, but most importantly in its methodological and theoretical orientation. As shown in Davidsen and Christiansen (2013), the single-touch screen affords a positive disturbance supporting the children's collaboration. This conclusion was brought to light conducting a micro multimodal analysis of the children's intersubjective sense-making. To put differently, the theoretical orientation and micro multimodal approach offered another interpretation framework compared to the experimental and design related studies.

To summarise, this multimodal rendering and analysis showed how the children make sense of each other's contributions through language, gestures and by utilising the material. The fragment of interaction also illustrated the children's perspectives situated in practice. The following sections deal with the challenges faced in the different phases of obtaining the children's perspectives in this way, and how it can play a role in helping teachers understand what the children are actually doing in technology rich classroom environments, and in the end inform the teacher' actions and design of materials.

CHALLENGE ONE

As stated in the introduction, the nano level, and particularly the children's perspectives, in ICT integration research is rather uncommon. Consequently, we decided to make use of video footage as a data source to capture the children's perspectives, as opposed to interviews, questionnaires or drawings. The primary reason for using video footage was to allow a closer look at the children's perspectives and grasp the nano level of ICT curriculum development. However, selecting and analysing video data with children's perspectives in mind has both practical and methodological consequences.

Selecting Video Data

According to Heath, Hindmarsh and Luff (2010), researchers began to use video recordings to grasp the participant's perspectives in the middle of the last century. Recently, the use of video footage has become even more common as technological equipment is becoming more affordable and accessible (Derry et al., 2010). It might seem of less importance to discuss the position of the camera, but in order to capture the children's perspectives it actually requires some attention. In this project, we positioned the cameras above the children to capture their interaction with the touch-screen. We decided to focus on the children, not the classroom or the teacher's instruction at the interactive whiteboard. With this camera position the children's gestures and use of materials was visible and the local microphone recorded their dialogue. In other words, the position of the camera framed our perspective on the children's collaboration.

In the process of selecting and analysing the data, we have followed the three principles formulated by Krummheuer (2009) when doing micro analytic studies: 1) Data analysis is based upon recordings of naturally occurring events; 2) The recorded interactions are transcribed; and 3) The analysis is based upon the sequential development of situated activities. In this project the three-steps unfolded as an iterative process between the second and third step. Basically, initial transcripts were orientated towards what was said, but as we experienced the importance that gestures played in the children's interactions we developed a micro multimodal transcription (see page 10-12) including language, gestures and the material at hand. As we are inspired by ethnomethodology in our selection process of the excerpts, we did not pursue any "probabilistic concepts of frequency and representativeness" (Derry et al., 2010, p. 14). Instead, the selection of the excerpts was based "on their significance and meaning within a narrative account" (Derry et al., 2010, p. 14). The selected excerpt for this chapter was chosen to serve as an illustration of how we render children's embodied interaction. Moreover, the micro multimodal rendering showed what this type of analysis can tell about children's interaction with touch-screens from their perspectives. The primary challenge of using video data to grasp the children's perspectives is not to capture video footage or to transcribe what they say and do, but to understand their embodied intersubjective sense making.

Video Analysis

In this research project, we applied micro multimodal analysis as a tool for a detailed study of children's "actual" interaction with touch-screens in peer-to-peer learning activities. This is based on methodological lines from conversation analysis (Goodwin, 2000; Streeck, Goodwin, & LeBaron, 2011), interaction analysis (Jordan & Henderson, 1995) and multimodal analysis (Norris, 2004). By combining these interrelated theoretical perspectives, we could explore and develop a fine-grained lens for understanding children's actions in touch-screen environments. To emphasise how children actually interact with touch-screens, we have produced detailed multimodal renderings to provide the most nuanced and context-dependent view from the perspectives of the children. The process of analysing the excerpt represents this main challenge in taking the children's perspectives. As Goodwin (1994) has showed, our professional vision influences our interpretation framework e.g. you see different things depending on your professional vision. In other words, instead of interpreting the children's collaboration supported by the touch-screen based on our professional vision as researchers, we should try to "bracket our vision" in our interpretation to see the situation from the children's perspectives. Hence, as we have argued throughout the chapter, the children's perspectives can only be obtained by orienting our analysis to how the children make sense in the situation. However, whereas conversation analysis, interaction analysis and multimodal analysis are oriented towards descriptions of *what* happens and *how* it happens, we used these two levels of description as a basis to inform teachers' knowledge of their own practice. Consequently, they can use this knowledge to design activities and materials based on the video analyses.

In summary, video analysis can provide a detailed view of the children's perspectives in a natural setting. Moreover, it is possible to study how the children make sense through language, gestures and the materials, which can inform teachers' designs for future activities and materials. Further, the video analysis shows that observations from practice provide another type of story than survey studies or experimental studies.

CHALLENGE TWO

As researchers of ICT in learning and teaching practices, we do not only aim to understand how ICT can support learning and teaching in practice. Hence, a basic activity in this project was to support the teachers' reflection on their teaching and learning through video feedback sessions. Throughout the entire project, researchers and teachers met several times for such sessions, during which the researchers provided the teachers with multimodal renderings of situations from the classrooms. Specifically, we provided short video clips with multimodal transcripts for every video feedback session. The teachers and researchers viewed and discussed these together during two-hour sessions. The researchers did not pursue a theoretical agenda during these sessions, but tried to facilitate dialogue between the teachers with regard to their analyses of the video clips e.g. their professional vision was sought on the excerpts. Consequently, we found treating the teachers as experts in their practice, with a unique knowledge of the children and activities, was essential to the approach. First of all, we find it important to stress the position of the teacher as a professional and not as an executor of a given curriculum. Secondly, we underline that teachers' opinions can provide important contextual knowledge to our understanding of the children's interaction. In other words, to validate our interpretation with the teacher's professional vision. As a result, the video feedback sessions facilitated mutual learning between researchers and teachers, and as a result the teachers became researchers of their own practice. To give an example of how this type of activity – "looking in the mirror" – can help teachers become researchers of their everyday teaching practice, we will briefly touch upon one of the teachers' blogs posted after a video session. Teacher Ben produced and shared a short video about how the video feedback sessions had changed his behaviour in the touch-screen environment. Initially, Ben moved around quickly between the pairs solving primarily technical matters, whereas he began to engage in a conversation with the pairs and ask questions about their work. Ben termed this as a transition from zapping around the room to a state of immersion in the children's learning activities. This illustrates how the detailed analysis can inform both teachers and researchers in understanding children's use of ICT in peer-to-peer learning projects with touch-mediated computers. By showing the teachers short video extracts of the children's interaction with the touch-screens, we mirrored their practice. Hence, we provided the teachers with an opportunity to replay what had happened in their classrooms. In this case, the teachers used these video extracts as a tool for reflection on action and design. To sum up, the teachers reflected on and revised their actions and designs. Furthermore, the teachers also confirmed some of the researchers' interpretations and added important contextual cues and information about the learners.

On a general level, the experiences from this project illustrate that video and multimodal renderings of children's activities can be a tool to allow teachers to become researchers of their own practice at the nano curriculum level. In Schön's (1991) terminology, the children's perspectives captured in the recordings became a tool supporting the teachers in becoming reflective practitioners in their own practice. Ultimately, the teachers obtained a "researcherly disposition" (Munn, 2008), recording, analysing and designing based on the video data collected in their classrooms.

DISCUSSION

An underlying question running through this chapter is whether the nano level of analysis has a role to play in the development of the future of schools, and as such in the field of educational research. The process of rendering and analysing children's perspectives is bound to the situation and context of the classroom. This fact is in many ways problematic if the aim is to generalise the findings. However, this kind of "co-learning agreement" (Wagner, 1997) seems to have potential for local and school-based curriculum development. Vanderlinde and Van Braak (2010) described a gap between the "world" of the researcher and the "world" of the practitioner. Overall, this gap is generated by a lack of shared language between research and practice. In contrast, the research and practice relationship in this project illustrated that video data has the potential to build a shared language, and possibly bridge the gap between practitioners and researchers. This can facilitate and develop better learning opportunities for children, because teachers have gained a more informed vision into what actually happens when children collaborate with the touch-screens.

CONCLUSION

In this chapter, we have highlighted the challenges and potentials of using micro multimodal video analysis of children's collaboration processes supported by touch-screens. Most importantly, the chapter shows how to conduct research on children's perspectives, and how it can inform both teachers' pedagogical thinking and qualify our scientific understanding of how children act in a digital 'learning space'. Working with video is in general an extremely time consuming activity, but it provides a situated perspective on how children actually interact with each other and with computers. Consequently, it is arguable that video provides a more real and nuanced understanding of children's perspectives than questionnaires and surveys, which can guide teachers' design of activities and materials in the future.

NOTES

[i] The names of the school and participants have been changed by the authors.
[ii] The transcription style if a modified version of the Jeffersonian notation style: pauses shorter than 0.2 seconds are indicated like this (.), longer pauses (0.3), raised voices are shown with CAPITAL letters, colon : indicates a prolongation of a word and finally ° indicates an audible breath.

REFERENCES

Blomberg, J., Giacomi, J., Mosher, A., & Swenton-Wall, P. (1993). Ethnographic field methods and their relation to design. In D. Schuler & A. Namioka (Eds.), *Participatory design: Principles and practices* (pp. 123-155). Hillsdale, NJ: Lawrence Erlbaum Associates.
Christensen, P., & James, A. (2008). Introduction: Researching children and childhood cultures of communication. In P. Christensen & A. James (Eds.), *Research with children: Perspectives and practices* (2nd ed., pp. 1-9). New York , NY: Routledge.
Crook, C. (1994). *Computers and the collaborative experience of learning.* London/New York, NY: Routledge.
Davidsen, J., & Christiansen, E. T. (2013). The benefits of single-touch screens in intersubjective meaning making. In N. Rummel, M. Kapur, M. Nathan, & S. Puntambekar (Eds.), *To see the world*

and a grain of sand: Learning across levels of space, time, and scale. CSCL 2013 Conference Proceedings, Volume 2 (pp. 10-14). International Society of the Learning Sciences (ISLS).

Davidsen, J., & Georgsen, M. (2010). ICT as a tool for collaboration in the classroom – Challenges and lessons learned. *Design for Learning, 3*(1-2), 54-69.

Davidsen, J., & Vanderlinde, R. (2014). Researchers and teachers learning together and from each other using video-based multimodal analysis. *British Journal of Educational Technology, 45*(3), 451-460.

Derry, S., Pea, R., Barron, B., Engle, R., Erickson, F., Goldman, R., & Sherin, B. (2010). Conducting video research in the learning sciences: Guidance on selection, analysis, technology, and ethics. *Journal of the Learning Sciences, 19*(1), 3-53.

Goodwin, C. (1994). Professional vision. *American Anthropologist, 96*(3), 606-633.

Goodwin, C. (2000). Action and embodiment within situated human interaction. *Journal of Pragmatics, 32*(10), 1489-1522.

Heath, C., Hindmarsh, J., & Luff, P. (2010). *Video in qualitative research: Analysing social interaction in everyday life.* Los Angeles, CA: Sage.

Heritage, J. (1984). *Garfinkel and ethnomethodology.* Cambridge: Polity Press.

Ivarsson, J. (2003). Kids in zen: Computer-supported learning environments and illusory intersubjectivity. *Education, Communication & Information, 3*(3), 383-402.

Jordan, B., & Henderson, A. (1995). Interaction analysis: Foundations and practice. *The Journal of the Learning Sciences, 4*(1), 39-103.

Klerfelt, A. (2007). Gestures in conversation – The significance of gestures and utterances when children and preschool teachers create stories using the computer. *Computers & Education, 48*(3), 335-361.

Koschmann, T., & LeBaron, C. (2002). Learner articulation as interactional achievement: Studying the conversation of gesture. *Cognition and Instruction, 20*(2), 249-282.

Krummheuer, A. L. (2009). Conversation analysis, video recordings, and human-computer interchanges. In U. Kissmann (Ed.), *Video interaction analysis: Methods and methodology* (pp. 59-83). Frankfurt am Main/New York, NY: Peter Lang.

Luckin, R., Bligh, B., Manches, A., Ainsworth, S., Crook, C., & Noss, R. (2012). *Decoding learning: The proof, promise and potential of digital education.* London: Nesta.

McKenney, S., & Reeves, T. (2012). *Conducting educational design research.* London/New York, NY: Routledge.

Munn, P. (2008). Building research capacity collaboratively: Can we take ownership of our future? *British Educational Research Journal, 34*, 413-430.

Nielsen, J., Dirckinck-Holmfeld, L., & Danielsen, O. (2003). Dialogue design – With mutual learning as guiding principle. *International Journal of Human-Computer Interaction, 15*(1), 21-40.

Norris, S. (2004). *Analyzing multimodal interaction: A methodological framework.* New York, NY: Routledge.

Orr, J. (1996). *Talking about machines: An ethnography of a modern job.* Ithaca, NY: ILR Press.

Roth, W.-M. (2001). Gestures: Their role in teaching and learning. *Review of Educational Research, 71*(3), 365-392.

Ryberg, T. (2007). *Patchworking as a metaphor for learning – Understanding youth, learning and technology.* PhD Dissertation. Published in: e - Learning Lab Publication. Retrieved from http://www.ell.aau.dk/fileadmin/user_upload/documents/publications/ell_publicati on_series/eLL_Publication_Series_-_No_10.pdf

Schön, D. (1991). *The reflective practitioner: How professionals think in action.* Aldershot: Avebury [Ashgate].

Selwyn, N. (2011). *Education and technology: Key issues and debates.* London: Continuum International Pub. Group.

Selwyn, N., Potter, J., & Cranmer, S. (2010). *Primary schools and ICT: Learning from pupil perspectives.* London/New York, NY: Continuum International Pub. Group.

Stahl, G. (2006). *Group cognition computer support for building collaborative knowledge*. Cambridge, MA.: MIT Press.

Star, S. L. (1989). The structure of ill-structured solutions: Boundary objects and heterogeneous distributed problem solving. *Distributed Artificial Intelligence, 2,* 37-54.

Streeck, J., Goodwin, C., & LeBaron, C. D. (2011). *Embodied interaction : language and body in the material world*. New York, NY: Cambridge University Press.

Suthers, D. D. (2006). Technology affordances for intersubjective meaning making: A research agenda for CSCL. *International Journal of Computer-Supported Collaborative Learning, 1*(3), 315-337.

Van den Akker, J. J. H., Kuiper, W., & Hameyer, U. (2003). *Curriculum landscapes and trends*. Dordrecht/Boston: Kluwer Academic Publishers.

Vanderlinde, R. (2011). *School-based ICT policy planning in a context of curriculum reform*. PhD Dissertation. Retrieved from
http://www.academia.edu/597620/School-based_ICT_policy_planning_in_a_context_of_curriculum_reform

Vanderlinde, R., & Van Braak, J. (2010). The gap between educational research and practice: Views of teachers, school leaders, intermediaries and researchers. *British Educational Research Journal, 36*(2), 299-316.

Wagner, J. (1997). The unavoidable intervention of educational research: A framework for reconsidering researcher-practitioner cooperation. *Educational Researcher, 26*(7), 13-22.

Jacob Davidsen
Department of Communication and Psychology
e-Learing Lab – Center for User Driven Innovation, Learning and Design
Aalborg University
Denmark

Ruben Vanderlinde
Department of Educational Studies
Flemish Fund for Scientific Research
Ghent University
Belgium

PART IV
CHALLENGES AHEAD

ØYSTEIN GILJE AND OLA ERSTAD

9. TRACING LEARNING ACROSS CONTEXTS

Methodological Challenges and Ethical Considerations

INTRODUCTION

When studying young people's learning activities across contexts in contemporary societies, it is almost impossible to ignore the role and impact of digital media, implying new methodological challenges for researchers. As this volume points out, it is hard to imagine how future fieldwork in educational studies can be "unplugged" from the digital realm. The authors in the previous chapters have explored and elaborated on different research methods, with the aim of understanding learners and learning in a wide range of contexts. As the readers of the volume have noticed, there are a number of methodological challenges within this field of research. In addition, there are ethical considerations that must be taken into account, given the fact that young people's online activities yield more data about young people's learning lives and meaning making than ever before.

This final chapter aims at understanding the complexity of following learners across and between sites or, conceptually, tracing, translating and reconfiguring learning across contexts. We will address some of the issues raised by the editors of the volume in the first chapter as we revisit some of the arguments laid out in each chapter. Beach (1999) argues that educational research has been dominated by two sets of studies on learning and learners. First, there seems to be a body of research looking at "learning in context". Such studies are usually conducted in a specific context: the classroom. Second is a series of studies of "context in learning". These studies pay more attention to how knowledge "moves" from one context to another. We will customise this distinction as it relates to debates on a specific physical place and a non-physical space, the online environment. With this point of departure, we might say that *learning in context* emphasises how research contexts have changed in educational studies due to digitisation in general and the Internet in particular. On the other hand, we might argue that *context in learning* foregrounds how learners perform agency in specific places and spaces as they create contexts of learning in their interest-driven activities. Traditionally, transfer are seen as involving the appearance of a person, in a cognitive sense, carrying the product of learning from one task, problem, situation or institution to another (Beach, 1999, p. 101). We will give a slightly different perspective on this "move" of learning experiences, knowledge, and identity in the last part of the chapter.

G.B. Gudmundsdottir and K.B. Vasbø (Eds.), Methodological Challenges When Exploring Digital Learning Spaces in Education, 135–149.
© 2014 Sense Publishers. All rights reserved.

To complicate matters even further, the Internet has created new dimensions of context as interconnections between online and offline activities (Nunes, 2006). These developments have given rise to a whole set of new research literature on the methodological challenges of studying learners and their learning across contexts (see Erstad, 2013, pp. 168-172). In our rethinking of the relationship between the learner and the context, we will argue for the importance, specifically within educational research, of following the learners and artifacts across sites and contexts of learning.

Thus, in the second part of the chapter, we deploy perspectives from digital anthropology (Horst & Miller, 2012) and multi-sited ethnography (Marcus, 1995, 2009) to explore how to study the learner when working in the digital environment and across contexts. To illustrate this viewpoint, we give examples from two Norwegian research projects: *Local Literacies and Community Spaces (Learning Lives)* (2009-2013) and *Knowledge in Motion* (2012-2016). In the final section, we discuss the ethical considerations related to tracing the digital footsteps of the learner across contexts.

EDUCATION, TECHNOLOGY AND CONTEXT

Contexts are addressed in a number of different ways within different disciplines, such as geography, anthropology, sociology, education, and computer science. Context repeatedly becomes a key issue in studies exploring the intersection between communities and schools or between online and offline settings, as experienced by children and youth. In the research literature, this type of blending of boundaries has been analysed in different ways using different concepts, such as "boundary crossing" (Akkerman & Bakker, 2011; Engeström & Tuomi-Gröhn, 2003), "boundary objects" (Star, 1989), "framings" (Goffman, 1974), "transformative learning" (Fisher-Yoshida, Geller, & Schapiro, 2009) and "seamless learning" (So, Kim, & Looi, 2008).

Within a sociocultural analytical framework, context has explanatory value, as it enables us to interpret and understand the interrelationship between learners and the circumstances they are involved in across space and time. In other words, a sociocultural approach pays attention to how contexts are negotiated in human interaction. As pointed out two decades ago, a sociocultural theory of mind "demands careful attention to the institutional context of social interaction. Culturally specific institutions such as schools, homes, and libraries systematically structure the interactions that occur among people or between people and cultural artifacts such as books or computers" (Forman, Minick, & Stone, 1993, p. 6). Following this line of thought, an important division in the understanding of context is presented by Michael Cole in what he termed "context as that which surrounds" and "context as that which weaves together" (Cole, 1996, pp. 132-137). The first implies a common notion of context as "all that lies around the activities performed" and pays particular attention to what influences activities in specific places. Such studies foreground an analysis of the learner, the task and the activity, while the institutional level, the communities, are understood as contextual factors.

136

This perspective highlights that "what surrounds" the learner influences the activities at the centre of the environment. Cole argues for another perspective on context, "that which weaves together", which foregrounds a dynamic rather than a static relationship between the activity and the context: "When context is thought of in this way, it cannot be reduced to that which surrounds. It is, rather, a qualitative relation between minimums of two analytical entities (threads), which are two moments in a single process. The boundaries between "task and its context" are not clear-cut and static but ambiguous and dynamic" (Cole 1996, p. 135, see also Luckin, 2010, pp. 9-18).

In the same line of thought van Oers (1998) criticised that basic conceptions of context such as "particularization of meaning" and "providing for coherence" depend on "cognitive structure" and the involvement of the person in a situation. He then presents an alternative approach to context, inspired by the ideal of developing a non-dualistic theory of human activity based on cultural-historical activity theory that denies the dualism between subject and object and states that the notion of context amounts to embeddedness in cultural activities (see also Duranti & Goodwin, 1992; Nardi, 1996). Van Oers argues for using the concept of contextualising rather than context: "Context, then, is the result of this process of identification of a situation as a particular activity-setting. Or to put it differently: the basic process here is the process of context making (which I will call contextualizing), which is an intellectual activity by itself, embedded in a current sociocultural activity" (van Oers, 1998, p. 482). In doing so, van Oers pays attention to *context in learning* rather than *learning in context*. To unpack the latter approach, we will look at the "classroom as a container" metaphor (see also chapter one).

As pointed out above, social and cultural analysis in educational studies have focused on how human activity is situated in contexts with boundaries. Leander and Sheehy use this claim as a point of departure in their discussion of space and place (see 2004 for details). Others have elaborated on these concepts related to learning and the use of digital technologies (Bekerman, Burbules, & Silberman-Keller, 2006). Even though Leander does not discuss digital technology per se, we think that his approach is interesting in our endeavour to understand studies of technology and learning in and across contexts. This approach pays attention to how space and place are dynamic and interrelated and must be assumed as embedded in and part of the activities and practices of learners in their everyday trajectories of participation, both face-to-face and online-offline (Leander, 2003). When paying attention to this dimension of learning contexts, we can find and understand more about how activities in contexts have spatial and temporal organisations. For instance, classes or projects across subjects in school have a specific duration, a pace and a rhythm.

METHODS AND METHODOLOGY – REVISITING SOME OF THE ARGUMENTS
IN THIS VOLUME

As pointed out in chapter one, several authors in this volume pay attention to how digital technology crosses the boundaries of learning contexts. However, there are a number of challenges in doing so. For instance, in the chapter discussing mLearning, the mobile phone is considered different from conventional learning tools that are designed for specific functions and contexts. Drawing on Peters (2007), Murphy and colleagues (chapter two) argue that mobile technologies may allow users to select *when*, *where* and *how* their learning activities occur, providing innovative opportunities for highly individualised learning. This fact might be part of the research strategy, as the phone enables researchers to *track learning activities across various contexts*. However, such use of the phone is very sensitive to ethical responsibilities.

In this volume, Burkle and Magee argue that educational researchers build more innovative and strong theoretical structures from which to understand the complex learning dynamics and epistemological frameworks that these virtual scenarios offer (p. 59). In their discussion about epistemic beliefs and computer games, they address two issues in research about the educational uses of games in digital learning spaces. First, they ask us to pay attention to the fact that methodologies within educational research are designed for a physical educational institution, not a virtual space like video games. Second, they point to the fact that avatars in games have an identity that can be flexible and contextual. This latter perspective drawn particular attention to issues around agency, and we will turn to this issue below.

Another challenge in researching learners in networked communities is the movement of people, texts and ideas across space and time. As Stornaiuolo and Hall illustrate, "this cross-contextual meaning making, which often manifests as resonances in networked contexts, remains difficult to address methodologically. Part of the challenge rests in understanding the varied and dynamic perspectives that emerge in networked spaces, especially the resonances that ripple and echo across multiple mobile and interconnected meaning making contexts" (p. 40). In such projects, there might be a risk of losing the "human" aspect of the interaction, understood as emotional and affective responses in these online interactions. Stornaiuolo and Hall admit that the S2C8 (Space2Cre8) network provided the researchers with a test bed, "a complex testing ground for exploring this cross-contextual tracing across online and offline spaces using multiple methodologies over time" (p. 40). In their collection and analysis of data, they realised after the data were collected that tracing resonance in recursive cycles might be well suited to meaning making's emergent and emotional dimensions.

The problem of dealing with a large number of data types is also discussed in a small-scale research and development project. Hatlevik and Egeberg discuss how to handle different data types, as they aim at giving feedback to the teachers after a project on the use of interactive whiteboards (IWB) in schools. Such a research approach is interesting in itself as a perspective on how to understand digital technology in contexts. In their discussion, they pay attention to the challenges of using different data and conclude that "it may not be possible to illuminate the same phenomenon through different observation approaches" (p. 91), particularly when the task is to give feedback to the teachers afterwards. The chapter by Davidsen and Vanderlinde seems to answer some of the questions raised by Hatlevik and Engeberg, as they look into a similar phenomenon, children's use of touch screens in classrooms. Davidsen and Vanderlinde (chapter eight) acknowledge that there are a number of challenges in using video data in projects where the aim is to give feedback to teachers, and they divide these challenges into two sections. However, they legitimate their approach by coping with the practicalities and the methodological implications in using video data for such purposes. They conclude that video data has "the potential to build a shared language, and possibly bridge the gap between practitioners and researchers. This can facilitate and develop better learning opportunities for children, because teachers have gained a more informed vision into what actually happens when children collaborate with the touch-screens" (p. 130).

These examples, derived from some of the chapters in this volume, point towards some of the challenges in this emerging field within educational science. As researchers, we must live with the fact that digital technology enables us to gather, collect and analyse data in new ways. On the other hand, new technologies provide us with a learning context where both researchers and those being observed and videotaped make experiences in a new environment. There might be a risk that we will end up doing research on a specific technology or constructed context, not the kind of learning cultures that emerge from young people's practices with new digital technologies. In some cases, this can be legitimised, as in the examples given above. However, as we have seen, there is no quick fix in how to do so.

We would like to move on from putting new technologies at the forefront to an ethnographic perspective on how young people actually use technology in a number of different contexts. This change in the focus pays in particular attention to learners' agency as they move within and across contexts with new technology available at the tip of the thumb. To introduce this topic, we might revisit Pribišev Beleslin's (chapter seven) historical approach to children's everyday life with computers. Pribišev Beleslin argues that research studies on children within sociology has been moving through four paradigm shifts. The first phase looked at children's use of computers in design experiments, while the next phase looked at the characteristics, properties and features of digital practices and children's behaviours in interaction with computers in natural settings. In the third wave of studies, researchers were driven by a need to understand *virtual* social interaction. This development led to a fourth paradigm with an increasing respect for the rights of young children, where the status young children shifted from "becoming human" to "being human" (Clark, 2010; James & Prout, 1997). This is an important shift underpinning attention to the kind of agency performed by young people in learning trajectories across sites. Pribišev Beleslin's argument is that we must pay more attention to children in their natural environment, the home, and related to this, we need to include in the research what parents say to address: "their perspectives on children's experience".

In chapter five, Donovan also takes the perspective of youth in a small-scale project reported on from New York. By inviting 11 interviewed youngsters to participate in a research project, these young people become co-researchers, and as Donovan argues, they gained new media skills and literacies: "Socially, they began to critique Facebook's long and complicated Terms of Use Policy and question what kinds of PII corporations and governments were aggregating, why, and how they were storing it" (p. 75). Such projects may contribute to a greater awareness among young people as they learn and make meaning with a wide variety of digital technology in different contexts. However, in doing this, the research project itself enables researchers to empower youth and perform agency in their use of social media in everyday life, as Donovan argues. These contributions both put an emphasis on children's and young people's agency as they learn in specific contexts, which are set up by the researchers. We will now continue to discuss questions of agency and identity as we explicate how to follow learners as they move from one context to another.

THE CONTEXT AND THE ETHNOGRAPHER

The debates raised by the authors in this volume resemble some of the issues around context or site explored in anthropology in the mid-90s. In the second part of this chapter, we will give two examples from our research building on ethnographical methods. In doing this, it is interesting to revisit George E. Marcus seminal article (1995) "Ethnography in/of the World System: The Emergence of Multi-Sited Ethnography". Taking into consideration the writings by Lefebvre (1991) and Soja (1989), Marcus argues that the study of social phenomena cannot be accounted for by focusing on one particular site. *One of the reasons* for suggesting this new approach within ethnography was to move from a conventional single-site location. Marcus argues for a new approach within ethnography that has the capacity to make connections through translations and tracings among distinctive discourses from site to site. *A second reason* for re-visiting the original term "multi-sited ethnography" is the interest in new modes of online communication within the field of cultural studies of science and technology. In regard to research methods, "multi-sited ethnography involves a dispersed field through which the ethnographer moves – actually, via sojourns in two or more places, or conceptually, by means of techniques of juxtaposition of data" (Falzon, 2009, p. 2).

As Drotner (2013) observe, the new digital culture is characterised by the co-creation of content and the co-creation of communities. This participatory culture (Jenkins & Purushotma, 2009) has been investigated by paying attention to the actual processes of content production and to a lesser extent the semiotic aspect of content creation (p. 50). *The last point* derived from Marcus' article is his view on modes of construction. He argues that research design in multi-sited ethnographies "define their objects of study through several different modes or techniques"

(Marcus, 1995, p. 106). Marcus suggests six perspectives on what to follow across sites. Among these is "follow the people", perhaps the most obvious mode of materialising a multi-sited ethnography. However, he also proposed an interest in following the artifact across sites. Building on this technique, (see, for instance, Willis, 1990), the connection between ethnographic portraits of the research subjects and the various knowledge practices that these research subjects are involved in across sites serve as a unit of analysis. Following the trajectories and pathways of the learner or an artifact is one way of reorienting studies on context in learning. This perspective enables ethnographers to trace and follow the flow of objects, texts and bodies that characterise this on/offline sociality (Dirksen, Huizing, & Smit, 2010; Murthy, 2008).

TRACING THE LEARNER AND ARTIFACTS ACROSS CONTEXTS

Multi-sited ethnography has been merged into the various new perspectives on how people move across space and place, both online and offline. In such an account, it is also helpful to make some distinctions between the different strands in this research, particularly to understand "where" the research takes place. *Virtual ethnography*, for instance, is research conducted completely "of and through the virtual" (Hine, 2000) and does not require face-to-face ethnographic work. *Internet ethnography* observes and analyses texts that appear on the screen without being able to meet their writers, while authors in *Digital anthropology* (Horst & Miller, 2012; Ito et al., 2010) argue that the digital is inherent in the physical contexts that young people move across. We will elaborate on this latter perspective among these new perspectives on researching the digital across contexts. Following this line of thought, we may argue that *connected ethnography* (see Sefton-Green, 2012) is based on the principles of multi-sited ethnography. This perspective puts an emphasis on following people using the entire set of digital media as a repertoire of tools. As Sefton-Green (2012) notes in an editorial to a special issue of *International Journal of Learning and Media* (IJLM), "The concept encompasses a way of theorizing and describing the kinds of learning that takes place in media ecologies" (2012, p. 2). Each of these concepts pays attention to the individual as part of a context, partly by paying emphasis on the context, partly on the learner (Sefton-Green, 2012). In this special issue, Vittadini et al. (2012) summarise the challenges in following the learner. They argue that the challenges related to this kind of research can be divided into four key issues: boundaries between online and offline experiences are blurring; young people act knowingly or reflexively; and their activities cannot be understood through the use of a single method but require the use of multiple tools of investigation. They argue that the methods used to study the learning processes and meaning making must shift from place to person. This means that we should take into account that the field investigated "cannot be anchored to a single platform or digital device but needs to be defined by users and their social relations" (Vittadini et al., 2012, p. 35). As we have pointed out above, digital technology enables us to follow the learner, but the technology itself is not a research methodology. We might argue that there is a gap between what the phone as digital technology enables us to do and how we actually can deal with the ethical issues related to using this technology in research projects. In order to overcome some of these challenges, we might use specific apps on the phone. For instance the MoViE app is a password protected mobile video sharing environment, which, enables informants to collect data and upload them on a shared database connected to a specific project (Kallunki, Penttilä, & Ojalainen, 2013). In the development of a research design, it is complex and difficult to combine methods that allow researchers to "follow" learners across and between sites or conceptually, tracing, translating and reconfiguring understanding across contexts.

Follow the Learner – The Young Gamer

The research design in the on-going *Knowledge in Motion* (2012-2015) project is qualitative and longitudinal. It involves two lower secondary schools in two different local communities in a medium-sized city in the densely populated (for Norwegian standards) south-eastern part of Norway. Fieldwork takes place over two and a half years, enabling the project team to follow developments from the second semester of eighth grade until the end of tenth grade in two lower secondary schools (13-15 years old). The main focus of the observations and interviews in a wide range of different contexts was to identify, describe and analyse learning processes in the domain of sport and media use. One of the boys we followed in this project is Oscar.

He is a gamer and an expert Minecraft player. Oscar is the eldest of two brothers, and he discovered the magic of Minecraft through his little brother, who started to play the game in 2009/2010. When in 6th grade Oscar started to explore the game just for fun, he could not understand the point. It took a while before he started to understand the logic of the game, the fact that he could build what he wanted. In the first two years, he played the game by himself. As a novice, he tried to play on shared servers with other, more experienced players, but he got "killed" because he did not understand the rules of the game. However, in 8th grade, he started to play the game together with friends, collaborating to build worlds on specific servers in the game, usually using the chat function in the game but also by talking on Skype with people he knows. Since he has developed as a player, he usually builds more sophisticated, functional buildings. We will argue that his engagement in Minecraft is an interest-driven activity where he has learned a set of skills and specific knowledge that are relevant for the game.

The aim of the project is to see how those skills, knowledge and competences acquired as a gamer out of school have any resemblance in the learning context in school. When we met Oscar for the first time, his practice as a gamer was "hidden" in the school context. As we followed the students into their Arts and Crafts lesson, Oscar's competencies were made relevant, as the students worked with a software package that enabled them to work with architecture. We noticed that Oscar immediately understood the principles in the software, and besides doing his own work, he started to help the other students in the class. This episode made us aware of his role as a kind of expert whom the teachers often addressed when they did not understand why the projector in the classroom would not light up or they had a problem with their computers at the teacher's desk.

In the subsequent fieldwork, we met Oscar in three different research contexts to understand more about his engagement in Minecraft and his identity as a gamer in general. First, as implied in the research design, we conducted interviews with all of the students in groups, talking about the two major themes outside of school, sport and the use of media. After this interview, we interviewed Oscar in a separate, small classroom in the school. Although this interview provided us with some information, which the introduction to this section is based upon, the lack of a screen with the object of interest became challenging for talking about Minecraft in detailed ways. The next interview with Oscar was therefore an online interview in which we used software to mirror his screen on our computer at the university and records this visual image beside the audio from our online conversation on Skype.

In this way, we could concentrate on the virtual environment, as in *virtual ethnography*, that he plays with. Before this interview, Oscar had sent us screenshots of some of the Minecraft projects he was the most satisfied with. For a final interview with Oscar so far (summer 2014), we visited him at home for a long afternoon. In this case, we obtained an impression of where he lives, his physical environment at home, and how he creates a physical learning context around his gaming activity. As pointed out above, Oscar played Minecraft just for fun for the first two years, he gradually became more fascinated by the hardware used in computers. We might say that his interest in the game developed into a more generic knowledge about computers, structured by his interest in reaching new "goals" in Minecraft. Although he does not attend formal education on such themes, learning about computers, he has "transferred" knowledge from informal domains, playing with his little brother and mates, into more formal learning contexts such as the event in the Art and Crafts classroom briefly described above.

Follow the Artifact – Enterprise Education

The *Local Literacies and Community Spaces* project is a large-scale ethnographic fieldwork in a community in Oslo (2009-2013), in which we followed three cohorts of children and youngsters over two years as they move from one educational context to the next. In the oldest cohort, we followed students' learning trajectories in Entreprise Education. In contrast to the case of Oscar, in this example, we followed a group of five female students (age 18-19) over six months as they designed a shim paper for sandwiches in plastic with the idea that this could be an environmental product that could be used over and over again. The shim paper, designed by the students, was produced in China and sent to Oslo as part of this project. This research study recognises and acknowledges the diversity in this expanding learning space where students draw on a wide range of practices in everyday life. In doing so, we followed these

143

learners as they moved within a wide range of different contexts over six months. However, on a weekly basis, we followed the project in classes at their upper secondary school.

Our first observations of these students took place in early December as they were joining a Venture Café, a special event hosted by Entreprise Education. The event is organised with a plenum made by each group, and then each group has five minutes to explain their idea to a professional tutor. These events were recorded in field notes, as we joined the table were the students sat and received advice from the tutors participating in the event. It was interesting to see how different the female students performed in this (research) context compared to the classroom. They had all dressed up and talked with tutors with no-nonsense chat as they very seldom had in their classroom.

Throughout their work, a wide range of different digital media was used to create and re-shape the artifact. As part of the competition, the students worked with a wide range of different software packages to create a marketing plan, budget, a flyer and a website, take photographs for the exhibition stall, and so on. The multiliteracies (Cope & Kalantzis, 2000) involved in this project were all related to the development and marketing of one specific environmental shim paper. Such a maker process, involving a wide range of digital media, is quite different from how students usually work in schools. In their work throughout the project, a wide range of media became tools for the students as they collaborated in the classroom, co-ordinated work with the producers of the shim paper in China, and took photographs and worked for long hours at their exhibition stand (see Gilje & Erstad, 2013 for details).

The methods used for tracking these activities across contexts varied. Generally, we made field notes in the classroom, and in particular, before deadlines, we video-recorded intense discussions of editing photos, making marketing plans and constructing websites. In addition, we audio-recorded long discussions in the classroom, sometimes with their teacher. We also took a large number of photographs. The photos allowed us to track how the "green idea" related to the environmentally friendly shim paper developed over time. In addition to capturing their discussion in the classroom and in other relevant places, we took photos of their model made in paper and cardboard (Gilje & Erstad, 2013). This artifact, presented for the first time in January, was a starting point for this learning trajectory, which includes observations and recordings of how the group worked at their exhibition stand in the regional competition as well as the national competition.

In this chapter, this story from an enterprise-learning context is just an example and not an analysis of how these tools mediated meaning and learning processes across time and space. However, this collaborative project explicates the ways in which students engage in the learning process by drawing on a wide range of practices in their everyday lives and resources at home. We might suggest that this way of collecting data over six months may illustrate how the learners' agency relates to boundary crossings over time in their making of a specific artifact that links between contexts. In this process, it is impossible to "unplug" the fieldwork from the digital realm, as the students in every part of the project used a wide range of different digital devices to organise, communicate, produce and edit their work.

ETHICAL CONSIDERATIONS

As pointed out by a number of authors in this volume, there are some ethical issues to consider when exploring the dialectical relationship between the virtual and the physical learning context. In the virtual context, there are also questions around how to situate oneself as a researcher in relation to the one being researched. This is particularly relevant in virtual worlds or in online gaming, as pointed out by Burkle and Magee (chapter four). On one level, there is a challenge in gaining access to computer logs owned by private or public corporations, and even after obtaining access, there are privacy concerns around adults and minors playing the games. Because gamers perform in a complex virtual world, a number of participants would not be aware of the researcher's presence and interest in the specific context. How should the researcher position himself or herself in such a context? Even though the S2C8 project was initiated by the school and set up by the researchers, there are issues around how to situate oneself as a researcher in relation to others. Stornaiuolo and Hall are concerned with what constitutes such public spaces, as they argue that "concepts of public and private spaces and texts are contested, and researchers face ethical decisions about how to situate themselves within these spaces" (p. 31). The personal technology itself, like mobile phones and personal computers, contains a large amount of user information. As Murphy et al. point out in chapter two, researchers can take advantage of this user information. However, this requires careful consideration of privacy and ethics: "Unauthorized disclosures or inappropriate use of personal information and location data could lead to embarrassment, marginalization or threaten rights to privacy and safety" (p. 19). As Burkle and Magee argue, even if the researcher records video and audio data from a session, "there would need to be a considerable amount of data-cleaning in order to distinguish which parts of the data were relevant to issues of learning and personal epistemology" (p. 51). These examples from half of the chapters in this volume address only a tiny part of what researchers must take into consideration when discussing ethical issues in their research.

In a recent article, Livingstone and Locatelli discuss the ethical considerations in this kind of research in a series of dilemmas. They mention a number of topics that the researcher must take into account "concerning informed consent, the relation of the researcher to research participants, the relation of primary (consenting) to secondary (involuntary or inadvertent) participants, and how to ensure confidentiality or anonymity in a digital environment" (Livingstone & Locatelli, 2012, p. 68). Livingstone and Locatelli note that there already are demands involved in conducting research on the everyday experiences of young people as magnified in relation to digital environments and established ethical norms for research with youth. However, "rather little guidance [is] available in relation to the further problems that arise when researching two crucial intersections: youth + online, and online + offline" (Livingstone & Locatelli, 2012, p. 68). Livingstone and Locatelli emphasise that the standard for the researcher in such studies is "to minimise harm, recognise the rights of human subjects, balance benefits and risks, and extend ethical consideration to all research participants at all times, including into an unknown future" (2012, p. 67). At the same time, their solutions to the digital dilemmas show that, in practice, this results in costs to the knowledge and insight that can be gained, as well as to the richness and authenticity with which researchers can document, report and be accountable for their findings. Moreover, they identify an important gap between the ethical considerations that apply to the moment of data collection and those that apply to the moment of data use: "In the digital age collecting large and rich datasets is increasingly easy, and consequently the crucial decisions are not only a matter of what to collect but increasingly also a matter of what to use and what to throw away" (Livingstone & Locatelli, 2012, p. 73). We have argued in the last part of the chapter that insight from multi-sited ethnography is valuable, as it, among other things, focuses on following the learner and/or the artifact. In a digital world, the challenge of tracing young people's learning trajectories across sites includes an awareness of the online context, even though the learning contexts investigated are physical places. As Livingstone and Locatelli argue, "in relation to youth in particular, it is becoming implausible to study the offline with no reference to the online (Ito et al., 2010; Slater, 2002)" (2012, p. 68).

FINAL COMMENT

In this final chapter of this volume, we have challenged some of the research designs that position young people in specific contexts, often providing them with new software or educational technology that they try to make sense of and understand during the same time as the research takes place. In such projects, the research design is determined by adults, but the research questions are usually sufficiently open so that young participants can implement them, also being unexpectedly stimulated by their lived experiences. Recently, a number of publications (e.g. Luckin, 2010; Selwyn, 2014) have suggested studying the use of ICT in classrooms in more integrative ways (see also Price, Jewitt, & Brown, 2013). Luckin (2010) refers to a gap between the researcher's knowledge and the practitioner's operationalisation of this knowledge in practice. In a similar fashion, Selwyn (2014) argues that a change in vocabulary is required to avoid a technical-oriented debate about the future of education and proposed that learners, teachers and others involved in the daily life of education should be given a voice in the debate about the future of educational technology (2014, pp. 5-8).

This implies that the research design must capture what is going on in digital practices to understand how young people communicate and negotiate knowledge in that particular practice. When researching digital lives and connected learning, we aim to understand how the participants perform agency when positioning themselves within groups of novices and experts across a wide range of interest-driven activities. This approach resembles what we have tried to illustrate in our two examples in the last part of this chapter. In doing this, we aim at exploring the complexity of following learners: tracing, translating and reconfiguring learning as they move across different contexts of learning in a specific learning trajectory (the enterprise project) or as learners through the three years of lower secondary school (the gamer Oscar).

The challenge is to build a research design that captures digital practices and the role of the informants at the same time. This is especially challenging in digital anthropology, as this approach is combinatory by nature and utilises a variety of research perspectives in the analysis of a given phenomenon. This is in contrast to a pure technical evaluation or a heuristic evaluation of the digital learning material. Hence, the overall argument is that this form of integrative research approach can provide a more holistic understanding of young people's learning activities across contexts in contemporary societies saturated with digital media.

REFERENCES

Akkerman, S. F., & Bakker, A. (2011). Boundary crossing and boundary objects. *Review of Educational Research, 81*(2), 132-169.

Beach, K. (1999). Consequential transitions: A sociocultural expedition beyond transfer in education. *Review of Research in Education, 24*(1), 101-139.

Bekerman, Z., Burbules, N. C., & Silberman-Keller, D. (2006). *Learning in places: The informal education reader.* New York, NY: Peter Lang.

Clark, A. (2010). *Transforming children's spaces: Children's and adults' participation in designing learning environments.* London: Taylor & Francis.

Cole, M. (1996). *Cultural psychology: A once and future discipline.* Cambridge, MA: The Belknap Press of Harvard University Press.

Cope, B., & Kalantzis, M. (2000). *Multiliteracies: Literacy learning and the design of social futures.* London: Routledge.

Dirksen, V., Huizing, A., & Smit, B. (2010). 'Piling on layers of understanding': The use of connective ethnography for the study of (online) work practices. *New Media & Society, 12*(7), 1045-1063.

Drotner, K. (2013). Processual methodologies and digital forms of learning. In O. Erstad & J. Sefton-Green (Eds.), *Identity, community, and learning lives in the digital age* (pp. 39-56). Cambridge: Cambridge University Press.

Duranti, A., & Goodwin, C. (1992). *Rethinking context: Language as an interactive phenomenon.* Cambridge: Cambridge University Press.

Engeström, Y., & Tuomi-Gröhn, T. (2003). *Between school and work: New perspectives on transfer and boundary-crossing.* Amsterdam: Pergamon.

Erstad, O. (2013). *Digital learning lives: Trajectories, literacies, and schooling.* New York, NY: Peter Lang.

Falzon, M.-A. (2009). *Multi-sited ethnography: Theory, praxis and locality in contemporary research.* Farnham: Ashgate.

Fisher-Yoshida, B., Geller, K. D., & Schapiro, S. A. (2009). *Innovations in transformative learning: Space, culture, & the arts.* New York, NY: Peter Lang.

Forman, E. A., Minick, N., & Stone, C. A. (1993). Introduction: Integration of individual, social, and institutional processes in accounts of children's learning and development. In E. A. Forman, N.

Minick, & C. A. Stone (Eds.), *Contexts for learning: Sociocultural dynamics in children's development* (pp. 3-16). New York: Oxford University Press.

Gilje, O., & Erstad, O. (2013, August). *Tracing learning trajectories across sites 'environmental thinking' as boundary object in entrepreneurship education.* Paper presented at the EARLI Conference, München.

Goffman, E. (1974). *Frame analysis: An essay on the organization of experience.* Cambridge, MA: Harvard University Press.

Hine, C. (2000). *Virtual ethnography.* London: Sage.

Horst, H. A., & Miller, D. (2012). *Digital anthropology.* London: Berg.

Ito, M., Baumer, S., Bittanti, M., boyd, d., Cody, R., Herr-Stephenson, B. et al. (2010). *Hanging out, messing around, and geeking out.* Cambridge, MA: MIT Press.

James, A., & Prout, A. (1997). *Constructing and reconstructing childhood: Contemporary issues in the sociological study of childhood.* London: Falmer Press.

Jenkins, H., & Purushotma, R. (2009). *Confronting the challenges of participatory culture: Media education for the 21st century.* Cambridge, MA: MIT Press.

Kallunki, V., Penttilä, J., & Ojalainen, J. (2013, November). *From video clips to digital stories – ICT in learning natural sciences.* Paper at the FERA 2013 Conference in Jyväskylä, Finland.

Leander, K. M. (2003). Writing travelers' tales on New Literacyscapes. *Reading Research Quarterly, 38*(3), 392-397.

Leander, K., & Sheehy, M. (2004). *Spatializing literacy research and practice.* New York, NY: Peter Lang.

Lefebvre, A., Herbeaux, C., Bouillet, C., & Di Persio, J. (1991). A new type of misfit dislocation multiplication process in InxGa1− xAs/GaAs strained-layer superlattices. *Philosophical Magazine Letters, 63*(1), 23-29.

Livingstone, S., & Locatelli, E. (2012). Ethical dilemmas in qualitative research with youth on/offline. *International Journal of Learning and Media, 4*(2), 67-75.

Luckin, R. (2010). *Re-designing learning contexts: Technology-rich, learner-centred ecologies.* London: Routledge.

Marcus, G. E. (1995). Ethnography in/of the world system: The emergence of multi-sited ethnography. *Annual Review of Anthropology, 24*, 95-117.

Marcus, G. E. (2009). Multi-sited ethnography: Notes and queries. In M.-A. Falzon, (Ed.) *Multi-sited ethnography: Theory, praxis, and locality in contemporary research* (pp. 181-196). Farnham: Ashgate.

Murthy, D. (2008). Digital ethnography: An examination of the use of new technologies for social research. *Sociology, 42*(5), 837-855.

Nardi, B.A. (1996). Activity theory and human-computer interaction. In B. A. Nardi (Ed.), *Context and consciousness: Activity theory and human-computer interaction* (pp. 69-103). London/Cambridge, MA: MIT Press.

Nunes, M. (2006). *Cyberspaces of everyday life.* Minneapolis, MN: University of Minnesota Press.

Peters, K. (2007, June). m-Learning: Positioning educators for a mobile, connected future. *International Review of Research in Open & Distance Learning, 8*(2). Retrieved from http://files.eric.ed.gov/fulltext/EJ800956.pdf

Price, S., Jewitt, C., & Brown, B. (2013). *The Sage handbook of digital technology research.* Los Angeles, CA: Sage.

Sefton-Green, J. (2012) Introduction: Innovative methods for researching connected learning. *International Journal of Learning and Media, 4*(2), 1-5.

Selwyn, N. (2014). *Distrusting educational technology: Critical questions for changing times.* New York, NY: Routledge.

Slater, D. (2002). Social relationships and identity online and offline. In L. Lievrouw & S. Livingstone (Eds.), *Handbook of new media: Social shaping and consequences of ICTs.* London: Sage Publications.

So, H.-J., Kim, I., & Looi, C.-K. (2008). Seamless mobile learning: Possibilities and challenges arising from the Singapore experience. *Educational Technology International, 9*(2), 97-121.

Soja, E. W. (1989). *Post modern geographies: The reassertion of space in critical social theory.* London: Verso Books.

Star, S. L. (1989). The structure of ill-structured solutions: Heterogeneous problem-solving, boundary objects and distributed artificial intelligence. In L. Gasser & M. Huhns (Eds.), *Distributed artificial intelligence* (pp. 37-54). San Fransisco, CA: Morgan Kaufmann.

Van Oers, B. (1998). From context to contextualizing. *Learning and Instruction, 8*(6), 473-488.

Vittadini, N., Carlo, S., Gilje, Ø., Laursen, D., Murru, M. F., & Schrøder, K. C. (2012). Multi-method and innovative approaches to researching the learning and social practices of young digital users. *International Journal of Learning and Media, 4*(2), 47-55.

Willis, P. (1990). *Common culture.* Buckingham: Open University Press.

Øystein Gilje
Department of Education
University of Oslo
Norway

Ola Erstad
Department of Education
University of Oslo
Norway

149

LIST OF CONTRIBUTORS

Tamara Pribišev Beleslin is an assistant professor at the Study Program for Early Childhood Education at the Faculty of Philosophy, University of Banja Luka. Her research and expert interests are pedagogy in early childhood, ICT and mathematics in early childhood education, preschool curriculum issues and teachers' professional development. On-going projects are: Media literacy – broadening the literacy competencies (overcoming the information overload) and theoretical and methodological problems of contemporary pedagogy in early childhood. Pribišev Beleslin has been a member of various expert groups in the Republic of Srpska and Bosnia and Herzegovina concerning national curriculum, pedagogical documentation and policy in early childhood education.
Contact: tamara.pribisev-beleslin@unibl.rs

Martha Burkle has a Ph.D in Technology Policies and Higher Education from the University of Sussex in the United Kingdom. She currently works as a Research Associate for the NSERC/iCORE Research Chair on Adaptivity and Personalization in Informatics Project, and as an Instructor for the Centre of Distance Education at Athabasca University in Canada. Her work has been dedicated to advancing research on the implementation of technologies to innovate teaching and learning. Her main research interests lie in the area of the use of virtual environments to engage learners' cognitive abilities, the use and application of mobile technologies for learning, curriculum development, online learning and training innovation, learning analytics, and the influence of virtual reality on self-identity.
Contact: Martha.Burkle@telus.net

Nathan M. Castillo is a Ph.D student and Research Fellow at the University of Pennsylvania focusing on the appropriate uses of technology for improving learning outcomes in Low-Income contexts. Castillo is currently supporting an impact evaluation of a multilingual, computer-based curriculum for early literacy development in South Africa. Prior to Penn, Castillo was based at Education Development Center in Washington, DC developing and implementing multi-channel learning projects through the use of interactive audio instruction as well as at-risk youth development interventions across Central and South America. From 2006-2008, Castillo was a health education coordinator responsible for teacher training and implementation oversight of a health and hygiene curriculum in the western highlands of Guatemala while serving with the United States Peace Corps.
Contact: ncast@gse.upenn.edu

Jacob Davidsen is a Ph.D student at the Department of Communication and Psychology at Aalborg University in Denmark. He is affiliated with eLearning Lab – Center for User Driven Innovation, Learning and Design. His research interests

are in the field of Human Computer Interaction, Learning Sciences and Multimodal Interaction. He publishes on these topics, both in international and Scandinavian journals. He teaches in subjects including "ICT and Learning" and "Interaction Analysis". Davidsen's methodological approach is within qualitative research methods with a specialty in micro multimodal interaction studies.
Contact: jackd@hum.aau.dk

Gregory T. Donovan is an Assistant Professor of Communication and Media Studies at Fordham University, New York. He has his doctoral degree in Environmental Psychology, Graduate Center of the City University of New York. His research interests are youth, urban and media studies; participatory action research; participatory design; social justice and smart urbanism; surveillance in youth environments; qualitative inquiry and analysis; social media and youth development; and the politics of information architecture. Donovan is currently co-editing (with Suzanne Tamang) a themed issue of *The Journal of Interactive Technology and Pedagogy* on "Media and Methods for Opening Education". He is also a researcher at the Public Science Project, founder of OpenCUNY Academic Medium, and helps facilitate cryptoparties, hackathons, and techno-activism events in the New York City area. He has previously held fellowships at the Center for Place, Culture, and Politics, the Macaulay Honors College, and the Stanton Heiskell Telecommunication Policy Center.
Contact: g@gtdonovan.org

Gunstein Egeberg is a Ph.D student at the Arctic University of Norway in Tromsø and a project manager at the Norwegian Centre for ICT in Education. Egeberg has lead research and development projects on teacher professional development and testing of students' digital skills. His research interests are in testing of digital skills, theoretical perspectives on digital competence and use of technology in teaching. In his Ph.D. project Egeberg is researching bullying, both in traditional and digital form, among students at compulsory education in Norway.
Contact: gunstein.egeberg@uit.no

Ola Erstad is Professor at the Department of Education, University of Oslo, Norway. He has been working both within the fields of media and educational research. He has published on issues of technology and education, especially on "media literacy" and "digital competence". He is the leader of a research group at the Faculty of Education, Oslo, called "TransAction-learning, knowing and identity in the information society" and is leading several research projects funded by the Norwegian Research Council. He is also leading a Nordic network of researchers on learning across contexts (NordLAC), as well as involved in several international networks and projects.
Contact: ola.erstad@iped.uio.no

Øystein Gilje is a senior researcher at the Department of Education, University of Oslo, Norway. Gilje explored in his Ph.D. thesis (2004-2008) how young people

construct meaning from visual culture when remixing with editing software. Gilje has edited a special issue of *Nordic Journal of Digital Literacy* (2012), and a special issue of *E-learning and Digital Media* (2015) on these topics, and his work received the new scholar award in the journal *Written Communication* (2010). As a Post Doc and senior researcher, Gilje has elaborated these perspectives in the research projects Learning Lives (2009-2013) and Knowledge in Motion (2012-2015), studying learner identity and learning trajectories in literacy practices across contexts of learning.
Contact: oystein.gilje@iped.uio.no

Greta Björk Gudmundsdottir holds a Ph.D in Comparative and International Education from the University of Oslo, Norway. She has conducted research in several countries in Africa on ICT integration in teacher education and the appearance of digital divide faced by schoolchildren and teachers in Southern Africa. Gudmundsdottir is particularly interested in marginalized and disadvantaged groups and their access and use of digital technologies. At present she works at the Norwegian Centre for ICT in Education in Oslo where she is a part of the cross-disciplinary research team exploring digital competence and digital responsibility by school children, teachers and student teachers in Norway. Gudmundsdottir is a member of the executive committee of the Nordic Comparative and International Education Society (NOCIES) and is a co-editor of the *Nordic Journal of Digital Literacy.*
Contact: greta.gudmundsdottir@iktsenteret.no

Matthew Hall is an Assistant Professor at The College of New Jersey in the department of Special Education, Language and Literacy. His research investigates the intersection of digital composition, multimodality, and collaboration. Hall is currently conducting research on multimodal feedback and its impacts on the disciplinary literacy of teacher candidates. He is a member of the National Council of Teachers of English, the International Reading Association, and the American Educational Research Association where he is active in the Writing and Literacies SIG.
Contact: hallm@tcnj.edu

Ove Edvard Hatlevik is a researcher at the Norwegian Centre for ICT in Education. He completed his Ph.D from the University of Oslo in 2006 with a dissertation about "Learning strategies and motivation among airline pilots". His research interests are learning strategies and motivation when students are learning with technology, and how schools develop leadership when implementing information and communication technology (ICT). Currently Hatlevik works on two projects. First, the Monitor project aims to identify use, experience and attitude towards ICT among students, teachers and school leaders. Second, the IDC-project (Identify Digital Competence) which is about how to identify and measure digital competence, based on digital competence aims in the Norwegian

curriculum, among students in primary and secondary school. Hatlevik is a co-editor of the *Nordic Journal of Digital Literacy*.
Contact: ove.e.hatlevik@iktsenteret.no

Michael Magee is a Ph.D graduate from the Graduate Division of Educational Research at the University of Calgary with a concentration in personal epistemological belief structures and video games in learning. His research interests include personal epistemological belief structures, learning in video games and simulations, transmedia design, learning analytics, mobile learning, leadership development and curriculum development. Magee's most recent research has focused on the cognitive and psychological impact of long-term use of technology. Specifically, the work examined the worldview of long-term game players and how that play affects their attitudes towards knowledge and learning. He currently works with the energy industry focusing on competency frameworks and leadership development to support the agile organization.
Contact: magee@graffiticomet.com

Katie Maeve Murphy is a Ph.D student and Research Fellow at the University of Pennsylvania focusing on policies and programmes to support Early Childhood Development and Learning in Low-Income contexts, and has recently completed research projects and field visits in India, Thailand, and several Latin American countries. Murphy is currently a lead technical advisor on an initiative to improve early childhood development in Western Kenya through the use of mobile phone applications for caregivers and community health workers. Prior to Penn, Murphy was based at the Earth Institute at Columbia University working with university partners around the world to launch cross-disciplinary training programs for practitioners in the field of sustainable development. Murphy was the Education Manager for the International Rescue Committee in Chad in 2006-2007, and was also a health, sanitation and education volunteer with the Peace Corps in El Salvador, where she lived for two years in a rural community working on projects related to health, education and income generation. She received an undergraduate degree from Johns Hopkins, a Master's degree in International Education Policy from Harvard, and a Master's in Public Health from the Perelman School of Medicine at Penn.
Contact: katiemaeve@gmail.com

Amy Stornaiuolo is Assistant Professor of Reading/Writing/Literacy at the University of Pennsylvania. Her research examines the academic, social, and ethical implications of online communication in global contexts, particularly as teachers and students integrate digital media into educational spaces. Currently, Stornaiuolo is conducting research on the social dimensions of reading and writing online, examining shifting notions of authorship as people communicate in public online spaces with global audiences. In addition to publishing and presenting her research in national and international venues, she is involved in a number of professional organizations and has recently been elected to the executive board of the Writing and Literacies SIG of the American Educational Research Association. *Contact:* amystorn@gse.upenn.edu

Ruben Vanderlinde is an Assistant Professor and Postdoctoral researcher (Research Foundation Flanders – FWO) at the Department of Educational Studies at Ghent University in Belgium. His research interests are in the field of educational innovation, teacher training and professionalization, and the integration of Information and Communication Technologies (ICT) in education. He publishes widely on these topics, both in ISI listed journals and more practitioner oriented journals. He teaches "Educational Innovation", "Pedagogy of Teaching", and "Early Childhood Education" at the bachelors and masters programme of Educational Sciences (Ghent University). Vanderlinde is methodologically experienced in mixed method research, and currently a member of the EAPRIL-board (European Association for Practitioner Research on Improving Learning). He is a visiting research scholar at the Curry School of Education (University of Virginia), and at the "Internet Interdisciplinary Institute" of the Open University of Catalonia (Barcelona).
Contact: Ruben.Vanderlinde@UGent.be

Kristin Beate Vasbø is an Associate Professor at the Department of Teacher Education and School Research, University of Oslo, Norway. Vasbø's research interest is youth life, learning and socialization in various social and multicultural contexts. Vasbø explored in her Ph.D thesis what types of learning processes and identification processes were activated through participation in international exchange programmes for young people. In the international research project Space2cre8 she explored the impact of media production with the use of Web 2.0 technologies on young people's identity development and learning processes in schools. As a Post Doc researcher in the research project Modernization as Lived Experience she explored identity constructions of young men and women in two contrasting societies, China and Norway, through a three-generational comparison. Vasbø is a member of the The M.A. European Youth Studies (M.A. EYS), a specialist consortium of European universities on youth issues.
Contact: kristibv@ulrik.uio.no

Daniel A. Wagner is the UNESCO Chair in Learning and Literacy, and Professor of Education at the University of Pennsylvania. He is Director of the International Literacy Institute, co-founded by UNESCO and the University of Pennsylvania (www.literacy.org), and Director of Penn's International Educational Development Program (IEDP) in graduate study. After an undergraduate degree in Engineering at Cornell University, and voluntary service in the Peace Corps (Morocco), he received his Ph.D. in Psychology at the University of Michigan, was a two-year postdoctoral fellow at Harvard University, a Visiting Fellow (twice) at the International Institute of Education Planning in Paris, a Visiting Professor at the University of Geneva (Switzerland), and a Fulbright Scholar at the University of

Paris. Wagner has extensive experience in national and international educational issues, and has served as an advisor to UNESCO, UNICEF, World Bank, USAID, DFID, and others on international development issues. He is a fellow of the American Psychological Association, the American Anthropological Association, and the American Educational Research Association.
Contact: wagner@literacy.upenn.edu

Fatima Tuz Zahra, is a Ph.D student and Research Fellow at the University of Pennsylvania focusing on policies, programmes and interventions supporting education for children and parents in low-resource settings. Zahra is currently conducting an impact evaluation of a teacher-training programme for local teachers that use mobile technology for teaching children from low and middle-income backgrounds in Bangladesh. She has also recently evaluated a health education intervention by Save the Children International in Jessore, Bangladesh. Zahra currently serves as an adviser at E3 Center, North Philadelphia, a non-profit organization that provides educational and mental health support to youth-at-risk and their families in Philadelphia (2012-Present). During her M.S.Ed. at Penn, Zahra interned at the non-formal education and literacy section at the UNESCO headquarters in Paris as a UNESCO Fellow. Prior to Penn, Zahra was based in Dhaka, Bangladesh and worked as a faculty member and researcher at the BRAC University. She conducted research on curriculum in the mainstream educational systems i.e. Bangla and English-medium schools and Madrasahs in Bangladesh.
Contact: fzahra@gse.upenn.edu

CPSIA information can be obtained at www.ICGtesting.com
Printed in the USA
LVOW04s0056210315

431460LV00003B/88/P